The Dance of
Intimacy

Also by Harriet Goldhor Lerner, Ph.D.

The Dance of Anger
Women in Therapy

The Dance of
Intimacy

A Woman's Guide to
Courageous Acts of Change
in Key Relationships

Harriet Goldhor Lerner, Ph.D.

1817

HARPER & ROW, PUBLISHERS, New York

Cambridge, Grand Rapids, Philadelphia, St. Louis,
San Francisco, London, Singapore, Sydney, Tokyo

FIRST EDITION

Designed by Alma Orenstein

Library of Congress Cataloging-in-Publication Data

Lerner, Harriet Goldhor.
  The dance of intimacy.

  Bibliography: p.
  Includes index.
  1. Women—Psychology. 2. Intimacy (Psychology)
3. Interpersonal relations. 4. Change (Psychology)
I. Title.
HQ1206.L446 1989   155.6′33   88-45519
ISBN 0-06-016067-5

89 90 91 92 93 TT/RRD 10 9 8 7 6 5 4 3 2 1

For Steve Lerner

Contents

Acknowledgments   xi

1   The Pursuit of Intimacy: Is It Women's Work?   *1*

2   The Challenge of Change   *10*

3   Selfhood: At What Cost?   *20*

4   Anxiety Revisited: Naming the Problem   *36*

5   Distance and More Distance   *52*

6   Dealing with Differences   *70*

7   Defining a Bottom Line   *87*

8   Understanding Overfunctioning   *102*

9   Very Hot Issues: A Process View of Change   *123*

10   Tackling Triangles   *143*

11   Bold New Moves: The Story of Linda   *162*

12   Our Mother/Her Mother/Our Self   *183*

13   Reviewing Self-Focus: The Foundations of
        Intimacy   *201*

        Epilogue   *223*

        Appendix: Creating a Genogram   225
        Notes   235
        Index   245

Acknowledgments

Although *The Dance of Anger* was a five-year undertaking, this book was finished in less than a year and a half. Happily, I have fewer people to thank.

My friends Emily Kofron and Jeffrey Ann Goudie read drafts on short notice, never failing to offer encouragement and good advice. Mary Ann Clifft generously put her editorial skills to use, going through chapters with a detective's eye. Other friends and colleagues responded to my call for help along the way; my thanks to Susan Kraus, Tom Averill, Monica McGoldrick, Jo-Ann Krestan, Claudia Bepko, Meredith Titus, and Nolan Brohaugh.

I am especially grateful to Katherine Glenn Kent for all she has taught me about Bowen theory and systems thinking during our many years of friendship. Her influence is reflected in all my work, and this book would not be the same, nor as good, without her. I am also indebted to the Menninger Clinic for providing an atmosphere that has challenged me to clarify my own ideas and to write. From the time of my arrival in 1972 as a postdoctoral fellow in clinical psychology, I have been blessed with dedicated teachers and colleagues, a superb secretarial and support staff, an unparalleled professional library, flexible work hours, and remarkably diverse opportunities for learning. All this, combined with my growing love for Kansas skies and the simple life, has led me to forgo Big-City living to settle down in the Midwest.

For the second time around I have been fortunate to be under the wing of Janet Goldstein, my editor at Harper & Row, who has influenced this book from start to finish, suggesting changes with clarity, delicacy, and tact, while respecting my need to proceed in my own way. I appreciate the careful work of the book's production editor at Harper & Row, Debra Elfenbein, and the fastidious copyediting by Andree Pages. My agent, Sandra Elkin, played a major role in making all this happen, and I thank her as well.

Many others have helped out in important ways. My friends in Topeka have closely shared my frustrations and successes as a writer, offering sympathy or champagne at the appropriate stages. Aleta Pennington and Chuck Baird have been generous-hearted and patient in the face of my computer anxiety. Jeannine Riddle worked beyond the call of duty when it came down to the final push. Betty Hoppes has facilitated my career from the start. Judie Koontz, Marianne Ault-Riché, and Ellen Safier have provided emotional support at home base. My long-distance community of feminist friends and colleagues has energized and sustained me through the best and worst of times. Countless readers of my first book have sent messages of overwhelming gratitude and affection, reminding me at the inevitable low points of authorhood that it is all worthwhile.

This book does not create a new epistemological framework for the understanding of relationships. Rather, I have worked to translate and bring to life what I have found to be empowering, theoretically sound, and useful in my personal life and professional work. In this regard I owe the greatest intellectual debt to Murray Bowen, founder of Bowen family systems theory, for the ideas and concepts that make up the very fabric of this book. At the same time, my interpretation and application of Bowen's work has been influenced by my feminist and psychoanalytic background, and by a worldview that differs significantly from Bowen and his colleagues at the Georgetown Family Center. For this reason, *The Dance of Intimacy* is by no means a pure translation of Bowen theory and as always, the ultimate responsibility for this work is my own.

It is understandably difficult to find words to thank those with whom one shares the most complex ties. I am grateful to my parents for all that they have given me throughout my lifetime and for being people I have come to so deeply admire and love. My sister, Susan, is an enthusiastic supporter of my work, and our friendship has flourished in our adult years despite geographical distance. My husband, Steve, has been my intimate partner in love and work for two decades; I thank him for his help with all my projects, including this one, and for our good life together. Finally, our two sons, Matthew and Benjamin, are a source of great joy. I thank all these people for what they have taught me firsthand about intimacy and for reminding me that being in relationships is a rich challenge indeed.

The Dance of
Intimacy

1

The Pursuit of Intimacy: Is It Women's Work?

I was cleaning my attic when I came across a poem I wrote during my sophomore year of college in Madison, Wisconsin. I vaguely recalled the brief attachment that inspired these lines—a steamy start which turned into an unbridgeable distance before either of us knew what was happening:

> Once you held me so hard
> and we were so close
> that belly to belly we fused
> passed through each other
> and back to back
> stood strangers again.

Neither the poem nor the romance was memorable, and my words certainly did not capture the anguish I felt when an initially blissful relationship failed. But I was reminded of what intimacy is not. And also what it is.

"All beginnings are lovely," a French proverb reminds us, but intimacy is not about that initial "Velcro stage" of relationships. It is when we stay in a relationship *over time*— whether by necessity or choice—that our capacity for intimacy is truly put to the test. It is only in long-term relationships that we are called upon to navigate that delicate balance between separateness and connectedness and that we confront the challenge of sustaining both—without losing either when the going gets rough.

Nor is intimacy the same as intensity, although we are a culture that confuses these two words. Intense feelings—no matter how positive—are hardly a measure of true and enduring closeness. In fact, intense feelings may block us from taking a careful and objective look at the dance we are doing with significant people in our lives. And as my poem illustrates, intense togetherness can easily flip into intense distance—or intense conflict, for that matter.

Finally, the challenge of intimacy is by no means limited to the subject of men, marriage, or romantic encounters, although some of us may equate "intimacy" with images of blissful heterosexual pairings. A primary commitment to a man reflects only one opportunity for intimacy in a world that is rich with possibilities for connectedness and attachment.

Whatever your own definition of intimacy, this book is designed to challenge and enlarge it. It will not teach you things to do to make him (or her) admire you. It does not provide guidelines for a love-in. It is not even about *feeling* close in the usual and immediate sense of the word. And certainly it is not about changing the other person, which is not possible. Instead, it is a book about making responsible and lasting changes that enhance our capacity for genuine closeness *over the long haul.*

Toward Defining Our Terms

Let's attempt a working definition of an *intimate relationship*. What does it require of us?

For starters, intimacy means that we can be who we are in a relationship, and allow the other person to do the same. "Being who we are" requires that we can talk openly about things that are important to us, that we take a clear position on where we stand on important emotional issues, and that we clarify the limits of what is acceptable and tolerable to us in a relationship. "Allowing the other person to do the same" means that we can stay emotionally connected to that other party who thinks, feels, and believes differently, without needing to change, convince, or fix the other.

An intimate relationship is one in which neither party silences, sacrifices, or betrays the self and each party expresses strength and vulnerability, weakness and competence in a balanced way.

Of course, there is much more to this business of navigating separateness (the "I") and connectedness (the "we"), but I will avoid spelling it out in dry theory. The subject, in all of its complexity, will come to life in later chapters as we examine turning points in the lives of women who courageously changed their steps in relationship dances that were painful and going badly. In each case, these changes were made in the direction of defining a more whole and separate "I." In each case, this work provided the foundation for a more intimate and gratifying "we." In no case was change easy or comfortable.

In the chapters that follow, we will continue to evolve a new and more complex definition of intimacy, as well as guidelines for change that are based on a solid theory of how relationship patterns operate and why they get into trouble. The courageous acts of change that we will explore in detail are "the differences that make a difference"—the specific moves we can make with key persons in our lives that will most profoundly affect our sense of self and how we navigate closeness with others. *Our goal will be to have relationships with both men and women that do not operate at the expense of the self, and to have a self that does not operate at the expense of the other.* This is a tall order, or, more accurately, a lifelong challenge. But it is the heart and soul of intimacy.

Caveat Emptor (Buyer Beware!)

I believe that women should approach all self-help books, including this one, with a healthy degree of skepticism. We are forever exhorted to change ourselves—to become better wives, lovers, or mothers—to attract men more or to need them less, to do better at balancing work and family, or to lose those ten extra pounds. There are already more than enough books in print for women who love too much, or not enough, or in the wrong way, or with a foolishly chosen partner. Surely, we do not need more of the same. Yet just as surely, on our own behalf, we may need to become more effective agents of change in our primary relationships.

Perhaps we should first take time to contemplate why tending to relationships, like changing diapers, is predominantly women's work. Caring about relationships, working on them, and upgrading our how-to skills have traditionally been women's domain. When something goes wrong, we are usually the first to react, to feel pain, to seek help, and to try to initiate change. This is not to say that women *need* relationships more than men do. Contrary to popular mythology, research has shown that women do far better alone than do their male counterparts and do not benefit as much from marriage. Yet men often seem oddly unconcerned about improving or changing a relationship once they have one. Men are rarely ambitious about improving their people skills, unless doing so will help them move up—or measure up—on the job.

This being the case, we might ask ourselves some hard questions. Why are women so concerned about upgrading their relationship skills, especially with men? Why are men relatively unconcerned? To understand the origins of this difference, let's look at traditional love and marriage, for it is here that the imbalance in "relationship work" is most conspicuous.

Women Are the Experts

I grew up at a time when relationship skills for girls and women were nothing short of tools for survival. The rules of the game were clear and simple: Men were to seek their fortune, and women were to seek men. A man's job was to make something of himself in the world; a woman's job was to find herself a successful man. Despite my own career plans, I felt it to be the most basic and immutable difference between the sexes. Men must *be* somebody; women must *find* somebody. Nor was "finding somebody" (to say nothing of "keeping" that somebody) a task to be taken lightly. The brilliance that my college friends and I put into our discussions of men far outshone what we put into our academic studies.

Today, women are no longer exclusively defined by our connection to men and children, yet we still remain dedicated experts on the subject of relationships. Although females may have some biological edge in our interest in and attunement to the nuances of interactions, the bulk of our wisdom does not come to us through the magical gift of "feminine intuition" which is carried on the X chromosome. *Rather, in relationships between dominant and subordinate groups, the subordinate group members always possess a far greater understanding of dominant group members and their culture than vice versa.* Blacks, for example, know a great deal about the rules and roles of white culture and relationships. Whites do not possess a similar sensitivity to and knowledge about blacks.

While women once acquired relationship skills to "hook," "snare," or "catch" a husband who would provide access to economic security and social status, the position of contemporary women has not changed that radically. Much of our success still depends on our attunement to "male culture," our ability to please men, and our readiness to conform to the masculine values of our institutions. In my own career, for example, these skills, and my willingness to use them, influence whether my papers will be accepted in professional journals, whether I will move up in my work-place, and whether my projects will be perceived as trivial or significant. Before the recent feminist movement, women depended entirely on men for the validation and dissemination of our ideas and for our definition of what was important. Whether we work in the home, in the "pink-collar ghetto," or at the top of the executive ladder, women cannot easily afford to alienate men or to be ignorant about their psychology. Even today, a woman who loses her husband will also probably lose her social status and her (and her children's) standard of living along with him.

Finally, our society still does not accord equal value to women without a male partner, despite the fact that a good man is indeed hard to find—even more so as we become older and more mature. Having absorbed the lesson that "half a loaf is better than none" (i.e., *any* man is better than *no* man), we may compromise our standards more than we are later comfortable with. We may then put our energies into trying to change him, which can be as energy-consuming as it is impossible. Pushing a partner to change is about as effective as trying to make friends with a squirrel by chasing it.

To say that our orientation toward relationships evolves, in part, from women's subordinate status does not imply that our feelings are misguided, excessive, or wrong. To the contrary, the valuing of intimacy and attachment is an asset, not a liability. Surely, women's commitment to relationships is part of our proud legacy and strength. The problem arises, however, when we confuse intimacy with winning approval, when we look to intimate relationships as our sole source of self-esteem, and when we enter relationships at the expense of the self. Historically speaking, women have learned to sacrifice the "I" for the "we," just as men have been encouraged to do the opposite and bolster the "I" at the expense of responsible connectedness to others.

Men's Lack of Concern

Men seldom become scholars on the subject of changing their intimate relationships, because they do not yet need to. Women often demand surprisingly little in relationships with men, whether the issue at hand is emotional nurturance or who cleans up the kitchen. We may settle for small change with a lover or husband and tolerate behaviors and living arrangements that we would not find acceptable or deem fair in a close female friendship. Parents, too, may expect less from their sons ("Boys will be boys") than from their daughters in the realm of communication and responsible connectedness, while children learn to expect less from their fathers. Until we are able to expect more from men in order to stay with them or continue business as usual, it is unlikely that men will feel called upon to change or even to pay attention.

In marriage, the gap between men and women in their attunement to relationships often widens dramatically over time. Dad need not notice that little Sam has holes in his sneakers, or even that his mother's birthday is coming up, if his wife moves in to take up the slack and handle the problem. Nor need he put much emotional energy into his parents' arrival for an extended visit if his spouse will plan their entertainment or make sure that there is toilet paper in the house. As long as women function *for* men, men will have no need to change.

Men often feel at a loss about how to become experts on close relationships, although their anxiety may be masked by apathy or disinterest. Many men have been raised by fathers who were most conspicuous by their emotional or physical absence, and by omnipresent mothers whose very "feminine" qualities and traits they, as males, were taught to repudiate in themselves. The old definition of "family" hardly provided a good training ground for developing a clear male self in the context of emotional connectedness to others. Men tend to distance from a partner (or get a new one) when the going gets rough, rather than to hang in and struggle for change.

Finally—and perhaps most significantly—males are not rewarded for investing in the emotional component of human relationships. In our production-oriented society, no accolades are given to men who value personal ties at the expense of making one more sale, seeing one more client, or publishing one more paper. There is a popular joke in my profession about the psychoanalyst's son who reports that he wants to be "a patient" when he grows up. "That way," the small boy explains, "I'll get to see my father five times a week!" Such jokes are told with barely disguised pride, not with apology, by men who are truly dedicated to their work. Let's face it, fame and glory do not come to men who strive to keep their lives in balance and who refuse to neglect their important relationships. The rewards in doing so can only be private ones.

I believe that for both women and men the most significant area of learning is that of understanding and enhancing our intimate relationships with our friends, lovers, and kin. Although I have chosen to speak directly to women, the subject is no less relevant to men, whom I also invite to read this book. All of us develop through our emotional connectedness to others, and we continue to need close relationships throughout our lives. Only through our connectedness to others can we really know and enhance the self. And only through working on the self can we begin to enhance our connectedness to others.

When we distance from significant others or pretend we don't need people, we get in trouble. Similarly, we get in trouble when a relationship begins to go badly and we ignore it or put no energy into generating new options for change. Fortunately it is never too late to learn to move differently in our key relationships. While in the short run the changes we make—and the initial reactions we evoke—may leave us feeling scared, frustrated, angry, and very separate, like many things in life it's a matter of sitting with short-term anxiety for long-term gain.

2

The Challenge of Change

At the heart of it all, this is a book about change. My hope is not that you will acquire a list of how-to-do-it techniques for "getting close," but rather that you will become more knowledgeable on the dynamics of change than you ever imagined possible.

Why change? Only by working to develop and redefine the self in our key relationships can we really increase our capacity for intimacy. There is, quite simply, no other way.

To Change or Not to Change

In our rapidly changing society we can count on only two things that will never change. What will never change is the will to change and the fear of change. It is the will to change that motivates us to seek help. It is the fear of change that motivates us to resist the very help we seek.

A story is told of a New England farmer asked to attend a forthcoming meeting at the county seat. The farmer asked, "Why should I attend the meeting? What benefit will I get from attendance?" "Well, the meeting will teach you how to be a better farmer," came the enthusiastic reply. The farmer was thoughtful for a few moments and then commented, "Why should I learn how to be a better farmer when I'm not being as good a farmer as I know how to be now?"

All of us have deeply ambivalent feelings about change. We seek the wisdom of others when we are not making full use of our own and then we resist applying the wisdom that we *do* seek even when we're paying for it. We do this not because we are neurotic or cowardly, but because both the will to change and the desire to maintain sameness coexist for good reason. Both are essential to our emotional well-being and equally deserve our attention and respect.

A Conservative Policy

While my own associations to the word "conservative" are not great ones, this word best describes my attitude toward personal change. Just as we strive for change, we also strive to conserve what is most valuable and familiar in our selves. And in a society where we are constantly being pressured to improve, actualize, and perfect our selves, it is probably wise to question why we should change at all and who is prescribing the changes.

Often we wish to get rid of some part of our selves—as we would an inflamed appendix—without recognizing the positive aspects of a particular "negative" trait or behavior. Few things are "all good" or "all bad." I recall a meeting of my women's group many years back when we had a little too much to drink and went around the circle sharing what we liked the *very best* and the *very least* about each other. Interestingly, what was labeled "the best" and "the worst" for each person turned out to be one and the same, or more accurately, different variations on the same theme. If *least liked* was one woman's tendency to hog the group spotlight, what was *most liked* was her energetic and entertaining personality. If *least liked* was another woman's failure to be straightforward, direct, and spontaneous, what was *most liked* was her kindness, tact, and respect for the feelings of others. If another's sense of entitlement and "Me first!" attitude pushed the group's buttons, it was her ability to identify her own goals and "go for it" that was most admired. And so it went. That evening I began to have a renewed appreciation for the inseparable nature of our strengths and weaknesses. Far from being opposites, they are woven from the same strands.

This experience also reinforced a direction I was moving in professionally. Early on in my career as a therapist, I deemed it my job to help my patients rid themselves of certain qualities—stubbornness, silence, demandingness, oppositionalism, or any other trait or behavior that seemed to make their life (or my work) especially difficult. Or perhaps I wanted them to be closer to their fathers, more independent from their mothers, or more (or less) ambitious, self-seeking, self-disclosing, or assertive. I discovered, however, that I could be far more helpful when I was able to identify and appreciate the *positive* aspects of what was seemingly most negative. Paradoxically, this appreciation was what left my clients freer to get on with the business of change.

Problems Serve a Purpose

Later in my career I began studying families, and came to further appreciate how negative behaviors often serve important and positive functions—even when these behaviors push others away or antagonize them. Let's consider the following example:

Seven-year-old Judy is brought into therapy by her concerned parents because she has temper tantrums and stomachaches and is demonstrating a whole variety of obnoxious misbehaviors. She is labeled "the problem" in the family—the patient, the sick one, the one to be fixed. Judy's parents hope that I *can change Judy* and rid her of her disruptive and self-defeating behaviors.

Upon careful questioning I learn that Judy's problems began soon after the death of her paternal grandfather to whom she was quite attached. The family is not processing or even talking much about this loss. In addition Judy's father has become increasingly withdrawn and depressed since losing his dad. His growing distance from both his wife and his daughter—as well as his obvious depression, *which no one mentions*—has everyone quite anxious. Judy's mother, however, does not openly address her concern about her husband or her distant marriage. Instead, she has increased her focus on her daughter.

When specifically does Judy act up and act out? From what I can piece together, this occurs when her father's distance and her mother's anxious focus on Judy reach intolerable proportions. And what is the *outcome* of Judy's troublemaking and tantrums? Distant Dad is roped back into the family (and is helped to become more angry than depressed), and the parents are able to pull together, temporarily united by their shared concern for their child.

Judy's behavior is, in part, an attempt to solve a problem in the family. It also reflects the high level of anxiety in this family at a particularly stressful point in their lives. More frequently than not, what we label "the problem" to be changed or fixed is not the problem at all. As Judy's story illustrates, it may even be a misguided attempt at the solution. And the "solution" we or others apply (which for Judy's parents involved increasing their focus on Judy and decreasing their focus on their own issues) just evokes and maintains the very problem we are trying to repair.

Small Changes

A conservative approach to personal change also means that we proceed slowly—and with the understanding that our moves forward will be accompanied by inevitable frustrations and derailments. Thinking small provides us with the opportunity to observe and check out the impact of each new behavior on a relationship system, and to sit with the benefits and costs of change. It also mitigates against our natural tendency to move in with a big bang and then drop out entirely when initial responses are not to our liking.

When an acquaintance of mine announced she was going to approach her father during the holiday vacation to try to "get close" to him by "breaking through his brick wall," I suspected she was doomed to failure. While I didn't know exactly what "breaking through his brick wall" might entail, I was not surprised when she returned home feeling grumpy and defeated.

The outcome might have been different if she had been less ambitious—if she had planned one specific move toward her goal. For example, she might have requested some one-to-one time with her dad, perhaps for coffee or a short walk. Because she and her father never had "alone time" in the midst of family visits, this in itself would have been a significant change, even if they had talked about nothing more than the weather. And had he resisted her efforts, she would then know she needed to begin with a smaller move still.

From a more conservative standpoint, it may have been premature for my acquaintance to make *any* new move until after she had taken time to get a calmer, less blaming per-

spective on the distance between herself and her dad. Perhaps she set up a confrontation that she unconsciously knew
was doomed to fail, because *she herself* needed to reinforce
her own distant position from her father, as well as her
perception of herself as the one who could be close. In any
case, breaking down someone's brick wall is hardly an example of moving slow and thinking small.

Substantive change in important relationships rarely
comes about through intense confrontation. Rather, it more
frequently results from careful thinking and from planning
for small, manageable moves based on a solid understanding
of the problem, including our own part in it. We are unlikely
to be agents of change when we hold our nose, close our
eyes, and jump!

Reassuring Sameness

Of course, it would be nice if we could make major
changes quickly—*or would it?* Babies and small children have
such an extraordinary capacity for change and growth, we
may well wonder why grown-ups can't hold on to it. When
my younger son, Ben, was six years old and my first book
finally made its appearance, I overheard him exclaim to a
small friend, "Do you know that my mother worked on her
book for *my whole life!*" It was true enough. And while I had
accomplished a great deal during that time, what had Ben
done in the same number of years? From a scrawling, barely
formed self with the most limited repertoire of language,
movement, and understanding, he had transformed himself
into a distinct six-year-old personality who was knowledgeable about some of the innermost workings of the New York
publishing world. Now *that's* change!

Later that afternoon a friend and I were musing about
how incredible it would be if adults could retain that extraor-

dinary capacity for learning and change. Actually, it would be a total nightmare, if you really stop to think about it. Our very identity, our sense of continuity and stability in this world, and all our key relationships depend on our maintaining a high degree of sameness, predictability, and nonchange. If we visit our father after a three-year absence, we count on him being pretty much the same person he's always been, no matter how loudly we may complain about the sort of person he is. In fact, we may count on this so much that we fail to validate and credit some real changes he has, in fact, made.

At the same time, change is inevitable and constant. No matter how effortfully we resist, no matter how hard we try to hold the clock still or attempt to view our world in static terms ("Someday I'll have my house/job/body/personality *exactly* as I want it and then I'll relax!"), we are always evolving and forever monitoring our steps in that complex dance of change. It is indeed a slow dance that we do with ourselves and others: moving back and forth between our will to change and our will not to change, between other people's desire for us to change and their anxiety and protest about our doing so, between our own wish for closeness when anxiety about isolation sets in and our need for distance when "togetherness" gets too sticky or suffocating.

When Relationships Are Stuck

The challenge of change is greatest when a relationship becomes a source of negative energy and frustration and our attempts to fix things only lead to more of the same. It is these times that we will pay special attention to in the examples to come. These stuck relationships are often "*too intense,*" and/or "*too distant,*" precluding real intimacy.

Too much intensity means that one party is overfocused on the other in a blaming or worried way or in an attempt to fix or shape up the other person. Or each party may be overfocused on the other and underfocused on the self. *Too much distance* means that there is little togetherness and real sharing of one's true self in the relationship. Important issues are pushed underground rather than being aired and worked on. Many distant relationships are also intense because distance is one way we manage intensity. If you haven't seen your ex-husband in five years and can't talk with him about the kids without clutching inside, then you have a *very* intense relationship.

Once a relationship is stuck, the motivation to change things is not sufficient to make it happen. For one thing, we may be so buffeted about by strong feelings that we can't think clearly and objectively about the problem, including our own part in it. When intensity is high, we *react* (rather than observe and think), we overfocus on the *other* (rather than on the self), and we find ourselves in polarized positions where we are unable to see more than one side of an issue (our own) and find new ways to move differently. We may navigate relationships in ways that lower our anxiety in the short run, but that diminish our capacity for intimacy over the long haul.

In addition, we may have a strong wish for change but be unaware of the actual sources of anxiety that are fueling a relationship problem and blocking intimacy. We are banging heads in *one* relationship, but the source of the problem is something we are not paying attention to, or do not want to pay attention to. We become much like the proverbial man who had too much to drink and lost his keys in the alley, but looked for them under the lamp post because the light was better. In Judy's case, for example, her behavior was defined as "the problem," but the anxiety in the family was actually evoked by an important loss. All family relationships had become distant because the grandfather's death could not be talked about and processed.

If we are going through a particularly painful time in a relationship, *that* is what we want to talk about and change. Our desire to focus where it hurts makes sense and sometimes we need to go no further. Frequently, however, a problem in one relationship is fueled by unaddressed issues —past and present—in another arena. Sometimes you can't become more intimate with your husband or boyfriend until *after* you have addressed something with your father, taken a new position with your mother, changed your part in an old family pattern, or learned more about the death of Uncle Charlie.

In this book we will be exploring stuck relationships in depth, as we follow the specific steps some women took toward a more solid self and a more intimate connectedness with others. We will see that changing *any* relationship problem rests directly on our ability to work on bringing *more of a self* to that relationship. Without a clear, whole, and separate "I," relationships *do* become overly intense, overly distant, or alternate between the two. We want closeness, but we become ineffective and fuzzy agents of change, moving in this week with angry complaints and distancing next week with cold withdrawal—none of which leads to anything new. Without a clear "I" we become overly reactive to what the other person is doing *to* us, or not doing *for* us—and we end up feeling helpless and powerless to define a new position in the relationship.

Our society places a great emphasis on developing the "I." Words like "autonomy," "independence," "separateness," "authenticity," and "selfhood" are popular if not universal goals. Yet there is much misunderstanding about what these words actually mean, who defines them, and how we can evaluate and improve where we stand on the "selfhood scale." Because mature intimacy rests so heavily on this business of *self,* let's take a careful look.

3

Selfhood: At What Cost?

Messages everywhere exhort us to achieve selfhood—to find and express our true selves. Perhaps a more candid response to this glorification of self in our culture is captured in the following incident. An aspiring young writer had spent long hours polishing up a composition for her sophomore English class, only to receive the grade of C-plus. "Be your *self!*" her professor wrote in bold red letters, underlining the word *self* several times. Underneath, perhaps as an afterthought, this same professor penned in, "If this is your self, be someone else."

Perhaps existence would be simpler if all the important figures in our lives could be that open and upfront about the contradictory messages they communicate. Most mixed messages are so subtle and covert that we are not aware of sending or receiving them. "Be independent!" is the spoken message we hear from a parent or spouse—but then "Be like me!" or even "Be for me!" may be the disqualifying communication. "Don't be so clingy," a boyfriend may tell us, as he unconsciously encourages us to express the neediness and dependency that he fears to acknowledge within himself. "Why don't you get your life together?" a husband complains, but when we finally make the move to apply to graduate school, he becomes depressed and resentful.

From the time we are first wrapped in a pink blanket, family members encourage us to be our authentic selves, while they also unconsciously encourage us to express certain traits, qualities, or behaviors and to deny or inhibit others. People need us to be a certain way *for their own sake*, and for the most complex variety of unconscious reasons. Throughout our lives, we learn that the survival of our relationships, and the very integrity of our family, depend on our being this way or that. We, too, unwittingly communicate such messages to others. Of course, learning what others want and expect from us is a necessary part of becoming a civilized human being. There is no "true self" that unfolds in a vacuum, free from the influence of family and culture. However, it is the *unconscious* or covert communications—those outside the awareness of sender and receiver —that often carry the most negative power.

The dilemma of defining a self is a particularly complex one for women. Because we are a subordinate group, our "true nature" and "appropriate place" have forever been defined by the wishes and fears of men. How, then, do we approach the task of carving out a clear and authentic self from the myriad of mixed messages and injunctions that surround us from the cradle to the grave?

At the simplest level, "being a self" means we can be pretty much who we are in relationships rather than what others wish, need, and expect us to be. It also means that we can allow others to do the same. It means we do not participate in relationships at the expense of the "I" (as women are encouraged to do) and we do not bolster the "I" at the expense of the other (as men are encouraged to do). As simple as this may sound, its translation into action is enormously complex. In fact, any sustained move in the direction of "more self" is a difficult challenge and not without risk.

For women, the emphasis on *selfhood* is a recent historical development. Selflessness, self-sacrifice, and service were time-honored virtues for our mothers and grandmothers. In contrast, we are now bombarded with messages that we should be strong, assertive, separate, independent selves, at least in the abstract. (In any specific relationship, such qualities may be less than welcome.) If we now fail to make use of the how-to skills or inspirational messages available to us, we may feel terrible about ourselves. Little attention is paid to the enormity of the task at hand, or even to respecting the good reasons why we may be unable to change. The story below illustrates one such reason.

"Dear Editor . . ."

Some years back, this letter to the editor appeared in *Ms.* magazine:

> It is with much regret that I must ask you to cancel my subscription. . . . Over the years I have enjoyed *Ms.* immensely, but for the last two months I've had to *hide* the magazine in my dresser drawer. My supposedly "liberal and understanding" husband believes the magazine is changing my personality, making me less flexible to his demands. In an effort to "save" my marriage, I am canceling the subscription. I feel like crying. . . .

"Here," I thought to myself, "is a woman with the will *not* to change." I clipped the letter and shared it with a small group of psychology students over lunch, inviting their reactions. The first student studied the letter and concluded that the husband was the cause of the wife's problem. The second student felt angry at the wife for giving her husband the power to make decisions for her—and then blaming him for it. The third saw the culprit as our patriarchal culture—the deep-rooted ethos of male dominance that affects us all. The fourth student chomped on her chicken salad sandwich and remarked glibly, "Well, there's a couple who deserve each other."

These students—two women and two men—differed in where they placed their sympathy and their blame. But as the discussion continued, it was clear that they all agreed on one essential point. We all can change and make choices. This woman does not *have* to hide the magazine in her dresser drawer, nor does she *have* to cancel her subscription to *Ms.* She could choose to do otherwise. That is, as one student added emphatically, "if she *really* wants to change."

Let's examine this assumption carefully, with an eye toward determining what might block this woman from altering her key relationship by changing and strengthening her own self. This understanding will help us to more fully appreciate the dilemma of change.

Now is a good time to pause and give some thought to the anonymous author (let's call her Jo-Anne) of the letter to the editor. How do *you* understand Jo-Anne's willingness to compromise so much of her self under pressure? What in her past history might have led her to this place and what in her present context might keep her there? What is the worst-case scenario—both in the short run *and* the long run—that Jo-Anne might envision should she do something different and clarify a position of "more self" with her husband ("I don't expect you to like *Ms.* or to approve of it, but I do insist on making my own decisions about what I read")? If the cost of change is high, what is the cost for Jo-Anne of *not* changing—of continuing in this same pattern over the next ten years? What adjectives might you use to describe Jo-Anne's personality or character?

A Problem in Context

Perhaps your reaction to Jo-Anne's dilemma is decidedly unsympathetic. You may see her as an infantile woman who enjoys being her husband's child and who refuses to grow up and take responsibility for herself. Maybe she even *likes* suffering and emotional pain—you know, one of those "masochistic" types who derive a secret unconscious pleasure from their victimized position. Or Jo-Anne may be downright immature, lazy, and unmotivated—unwilling to put forth the effort that change requires. If we keep a narrow spotlight on Jo-Anne and view the problem as existing entirely under her skin, these are the kind of interpretations we are likely to come up with.

Suppose instead, we are able to view Jo-Anne's problem in a broader context and examine her situation through a wide-angle lens. *Would any of the following facts make a difference in how you understand her decision to hide* Ms. *from her husband and ultimately cancel her subscription?*

Would it make a difference if Jo-Anne was a middle-aged woman with three dependent children, little formal education, and no support systems or marketable skills? Would it make a difference to know that changes in the direction of "more self" would be intolerable enough to her husband that he would ultimately leave her? Does Jo-Anne's resistance to change make more sense if we know that she is quite literally one husband away from a welfare check?

Would it make a difference if this husband's apparent good functioning rests on Jo-Anne's poor functioning—that whenever *she* begins to look better, he begins to look worse? Does it make a difference to know that her husband has a history of violent behavior, as well as severe depression —but that he has been functioning well since Jo-Anne has moved into a more accommodating, submissive role in their marriage?

Would it make a difference if in Jo-Anne's first family there was a powerful taboo against expressing differences, and that early in life Jo-Anne learned that asserting the "I" would threaten the most important family relationships on which she depended totally?

Would it make a difference to know that in canceling her subscription to *Ms.* magazine, Jo-Anne is doing exactly what women in her family have done for at least three hundred years? That accommodating to one's husband is a deep-rooted family tradition that links Jo-Anne to the important women in her past? That for Jo-Anne to do otherwise, or differently, would be to challenge the very "reality" of generations of women in her family and would constitute, at least unconsciously, a betrayal—a loss of identity and meaning?

Does any of this information, these small additional pieces of a much larger picture, change or inform your personal reaction to Jo-Anne's decision to cancel her subscription to *Ms.*? Or do you think, like the psychology students, that Jo-Anne could certainly make a change within her marriage "if she *really* wanted to change"?

How Much We Don't Know

All of us are psychologists of sorts, even if this is not our trade. When we are not able to make a desired change, we will construct an explanation to make sense of our painful experience. We may diagnose ourselves ("I'm scared of my sexuality, that's why I can't lose weight") or the other person ("He just can't deal with intimacy"). We may blame our mothers, our genes, our hormones, or the stars, but in each case our understanding of the problem is just a small piece of the elephant.

We actually know very little about the strong human will not to change. If Jo-Anne were to go to ten therapists—and then resist their efforts to help her become a more assertive person—she would probably be on the receiving end of ten different interpretations. Each interpretation would be based on the therapist's own particular theory or belief system about Jo-Anne's resistance to change. All these theories and interpretations might be wrong. Or all might be correct, with each representing a small part of a much larger and more complicated picture. We are encouraged to accept "expert advice" as truth, when in reality a great deal about human behavior is unknown.

Perhaps the best truth we have is that no expert can know with 100 percent certainty what is best for Jo-Anne at a particular point in time or what changes she can tolerate. On the one hand, the costs of *non*change are often clearly apparent. For Jo-Anne, these costs may include chronic anger and bitterness, feelings of depression, anxiety, low self-esteem, or even self-hatred. They may include sexual or work inhibitions, physical complaints, or any other symptom in the book. We *do* know there is a price we pay when we betray and sacrifice the self, when too much of the self becomes negotiable under relationship pressures.

What is far more difficult to determine—what we cannot know completely or with certainty—is the price Jo-Anne would have to pay for change at this time. In fact, Jo-Anne herself can only begin to know this *after* she makes a change ("I will choose what I read in this marriage, whether you approve of it or not") and as she *holds to her decision* through the inevitable turmoil and anxiety that such a change inevitably evokes. As Margaret Mead so aptly pointed out, the disruption caused by change can only be solved by *more change,* and so one thing leads to another. If Jo-Anne decides she will *not* cancel her subscription to *Ms.,* she will begin to feel an internal pressure to take a position on other issues that are important to her. As the old marital equilibrium is disrupted, her husband will also be called upon to change. How much change can these two, as individuals and as a couple, manage over time? The answer is that we do not know.

Change requires courage, but the failure to change does not signify the lack of it. Women are quick to blame themselves—and to be blamed by others—when we are not able to make the changes that we ourselves seek or that others prescribe for us. We fail to respect the wisdom of the unconscious, which may tell us "No!" as our conscious mind says "Go!"

Keep in mind how little even the experts know about the process of change. And remember also that even the most self-defeating and problematic behavior patterns may exist for a good reason. We saw this in the brief example of seven-year-old Judy (Chapter 1). Here is a firsthand account.

The Will Not to Change: A Personal Story

When I was twelve years old, my mother was diagnosed with advanced endometrial cancer. Earlier symptoms of the disease had been misdiagnosed as menopause, and when the correct diagnosis was finally made, she was given a very poor prognosis. This was in the fifties, a time when children were typically "protected" from such painful information through secrecy and silence. No facts were provided about my mother's health problem, although it seemed obvious that she was dying. The level of anxiety in my family was chronically high, but the source of the anxiety was not mentioned. The word "cancer" was never spoken.

My older sister, Susan (a typical firstborn), managed her anxiety by *overfunctioning*, and I (a typical youngest) managed my anxiety by *underfunctioning*. Over time our positions became polarized and rigidly entrenched. The more my sister overfunctioned the more I underfunctioned, and vice versa. Here's how it went.

Susan, then a freshman at Barnard College, traveled three hours each day on the subway between Brooklyn and Manhattan, returning home to organize and take care of the entire household. She cooked, cleaned, ironed, and did everything that needed to be done with perfect competence and without complaint. If she felt scared, vulnerable, angry, or unhappy, she hid these feelings, even from herself. I, on the other hand, expressed enough of these feelings for the entire family. I became as bad as she was good—creating various scenes, making impossible demands for clothes that my family could not afford, and messing things up as quickly as my sister was able to clean and straighten them. I acted up in school and my parents were informed that I would never be "college material."

My father distanced (a typical male pattern of managing stress) and my mother handled her anxiety by *focusing on me.* Indeed, about 98 percent of her worry energy went in my direction. She became concerned, if not preoccupied, with the thought that I would not make it if she died. (Susan, she concluded, would do just fine.) My mother, who has always prided herself on being a "fighter" and a "survivor," decided that *for my sake,* she could not die. And die she did not. Even today (as I write this, she is pushing eighty), my mother does not hesitate for a moment when she is asked how she stayed alive against all medical odds. "You see," she explains, as if the answer is perfectly logical and merits no further explanation, "I could not die at that time. Harriet needed me. She was such a mess!"

A mess I was—and an incorrigible one at that. I was sent to a psychotherapist who did his best to straighten me out, but my unconscious will *not* to change was stronger than his best efforts to offer help. I remained a mess until I felt more confident that my mother was out of the woods.

Did my being a mess keep my mother alive? Recently, I called her in Phoenix and put this question to her directly. Now that our family is able to talk much more openly about difficult emotional issues, I continue to process this painful period of my life in a way that was not possible at the time. I asked my mother whether she *truly* believed that it was my being a mess that allowed her to live. Would she *actually* have died—as she now sees it—had I given her the impression that I was doing just fine?

My mother's most honest and thoughtful reaction was to say that looking back, she really was not sure. When the cancer was diagnosed, she had "no self"; although she could give and do for her children, she could not give and do on her own behalf. At first, she explained, she was fighting the cancer 80 percent for me, and 20 percent for herself. Over time, the balance began to shift as my mother learned to value her own life and make it a priority.

Did my being a mess *really* allow my mother to survive? We cannot know for sure. I am confident, however, of one thing. At some unconscious level, this twelve-year-old child believed it was my job in the family to keep my mother alive by being a mess. I believed this as deeply as my sister, Susan, believed that the integrity of the family depended on her being the all-good, all-responsible daughter who would hide any sign of vulnerability and pain. I was steadfast in my unconscious determination to resist all efforts to help me shape up. And sadly, we did not have the kind of help that our family actually needed, help that would have made it possible for all four of us to process my mother's cancer in a more open and direct way.

I have shared this story with you, and asked you to reflect on one woman's letter to the editor, in the hope that you will approach your own attempts at change with patience. The ideas and suggestions that lie ahead will be most useful to you if you can greet them with an open, courageous, and experimental attitude. But also keep in mind that no one else can tell you what changes you *should* make, at what speed, and at what cost. No expert, not even your therapist, can know for certain when it is the right time for you to change, how much change is tolerable and in what doses, and how various moves forward and backward will affect your emotional well-being, your relationships, your sense of self, your moorings in this world, and your (or someone else's) immune system.

Fortunately, the unconscious is very wise. What you read in this book will always be there for you—long after you think you have forgotten it—until the time is right for you to make use of it. Respect the fact that all you do and are now, has evolved for a good reason and serves an important purpose. Trust your own way more than the experts who promote change, myself included, because ultimately you are the best expert on your own self.

Selfhood or De-Selfing: Defining Our Terms

If our capacity for intimacy rests first and foremost on our continued efforts to be *more of a self,* how can we judge where we are on the "selfhood scale"? How can we measure the degree to which we are able to carve out a separate, whole, independent self within our closest relationships? Whether we call it "selfhood" or prefer a different word, such as "autonomy" or "independence," what are the criteria for having a lot of it—or not very much? Before reading on, you might want to jot down your own standards of measurement. How do *you* define it? Exactly what do you mean when you say, "She (or he) is a *very* independent person!"

Let me begin by sharing what I do *not* mean when I use these words. I do *not* mean, "She sits on the board of General Motors." I do *not* mean, "He really doesn't seem to need other people very much." I do *not* mean, "She doesn't care what other people think of her." I do *not* mean, "He has it all together—no problems." These statements refer more to *pseudo-independence* than to real self. We *all* need people, we are *all* deeply affected by how other people treat us. No one is without vulnerability, anxieties, and problems. And despite its rewards, there is nothing particularly "independent" about moving up the ladder of success. In fact, success in the public domain may require a high degree of conformity and sacrifice of personal values.

If, however, we have come to believe that such is the *real stuff* of which independence or selfhood is made, then men may appear to have far more of it than women. That's not the case. What *is* the case is that many men have more *pseudo-self* or *pseudo-independence,* often acquired at the expense of others: women, children, and less powerful men.

How, then, can we think in a more objective way about this business of "self"? How do we begin to define our terms?

What's "Low" on the Selfhood Scale?

Jo-Anne's letter to the editor provides us with an obvious example of a couple that is operating at the low end of the selfhood scale. Her husband, we can assume, is threatened by the emergence of *differences* in their relationship and by his wife's own growth. His position of dominance (being the one who makes the rules in the relationship) may give him a sense of pseudo-self (or pseudo-independence), but this rests on his wife's one-down, accommodating stance. Jo-Anne, for her part, sacrifices a great deal of self in her marriage. Surely, subscribing to *Ms.* is not the only issue in their relationship on which she fails to take a stand and thus behaves in ways that are not congruent with her own beliefs and values. This is not to say that this couple's behavior is without sense or reason. In fact, this marital dance is an exaggeration of one that is encouraged and prescribed in our culture and held in place by social and economic arrangements. But it is probably clear to even the casual reader that neither husband nor wife would rate at the top of the selfhood scale.

There are other ways in which we sacrifice or lose self that are less obvious to observe or label. When anxiety is high, and particularly if it remains high over a long period of time, *we are likely to get into extreme positions in relationships where the self is out of balance, and our relationships become polarized.* Consider how my own family operated during the period of high stress following the diagnosis of my mother's cancer.

For starters, my own role as "the mess" in the family, or "the problem child," was a de-selfed position. I was not able to free myself from the anxious, emotional family field in order to make use of my competence and show my strong, positive side to others. Like Jo-Anne, I believed that the integrity of my relationships, perhaps my very survival, depended on my giving up self. Unlike Jo-Anne, I could not have articulated my dilemma. I did not *consciously* give up self, as she did.

What about my sister? She behaved so competently, maturely, and responsibly—and so clearly seemed to have it all together—that surely *she* would be high on the selfhood scale. That's how others saw it, including my parents, who viewed Susan as sailing through the crisis. And yet Susan's overfunctioning behavior was as de-selfed as my own under-functioning behavior. She was no higher on the selfhood scale, she was only sitting on the opposite end of the seesaw. All of us have a vulnerable side, just as all of us have strength and competence. When we cannot express *both* sides with some balance, then we are not operating with a whole and authentic self.

What about my father? Like many men, he distanced. This may have been his attempt at helping the family, and certainly at lowering his own anxiety. Distant people are often labeled as "having no feelings," but *distancing is actually a way of managing very intense feelings.* It is also a de-selfed position. We are not high on the selfhood scale when we cannot stay emotionally connected to family members and speak directly to the important and difficult issues in our lives.

And my mother? By her own report she did not have enough self to choose life on her own behalf. My mother can now speak eloquently about how the cancer (and a trip to the Grand Canyon) challenged her to be her self and to be *for* her self. But this came later. Also, focusing on a child (or on any other family member) is another way that we manage anxiety, but at cost to both the self and the focused-on individual.

Toward More Self

It is not my intention to portray my family as a neurotic group of nonselves. Quite the contrary. My mother, father, sister, and I were simply behaving as individuals and families behave under stress. *Overfunctioning, underfunctioning, fighting, pursuing, distancing,* and *child-focus* (or *other-focus*) are normal, patterned ways to manage anxiety. One way is not better or more virtuous than another.

But when anxiety is high enough or lasts long enough, we get locked into rigid and extreme positions on these dimensions. Then our relationships become polarized and stuck, and we may have difficulty finding creative new options for our own behavior. In fact, the very things that we do to lower our anxiety usually just keep the old pattern going, blocking any possibility of intimacy. And the actual sources of the anxiety may be unclear or difficult for us to focus on and process.

When this kind of stalemate occurs, we need to work on the "I," and always in the direction of movement toward "more self." You may already have some idea of what this work entails. We move up on the selfhood scale (and the intimacy scale, for that matter) when we are able to:

- present a balanced picture of both our strengths and our vulnerabilities.
- make clear statements of our beliefs, values, and priorities, and then keep our behavior congruent with these.
- stay emotionally connected to significant others even when things get pretty intense.
- address difficult and painful issues and take a position on matters important to us.
- state our differences and allow others to do the same.

This is not *all* that "being a self" involves, but it's a good start. And it is the very stuff that intimacy is made of.

In the chapters that follow, we will see how moves toward intimacy always require us to focus on the self as the primary vehicle for change, while viewing the self in the broadest possible context. This is a difficult task in the best of circumstances. When anxiety is high, it is more difficult still.

4

Anxiety Revisited: Naming the Problem

"Anxiety is the pits!" I recently remarked to a close friend. I was having more than my fair share of it at the time. My friend, in her cheerful attempt to add perspective, reminded me that people don't die from anxiety—and that eventually it goes away. That was not a bad reminder. Anxiety can make you shake, lose sleep, feel dizzy or nauseous. It can convince you that you are losing your memory, if not your mind. But anxiety is rarely fatal. And eventually it will subside.

Of course, this is not the whole story. The things we do to *avoid* the experience of anxiety, and the particular patterned ways we *react* to it, may keep our relationships, and our selves, painfully stuck. What's reflexive and adaptive in the short run may carry the highest price tag over time. Even over generations.

The initial impact of anxiety on a relationship is always one of increased reactivity. Reactivity is an automatic, anxiety-driven response. When we are in reactive gear, we are driven by our feelings, without the ability to think about how we want to express them. In fact, we cannot think about the self or our relationships with much objectivity at all. We sincerely want things to be calmer and more intimate, but we keep reflexively doing what we always do, which only leads to more of the same.

Whatever our style of navigating key relationships under stress—pursuing, distancing, fighting, child-focus, overfunctioning, underfunctioning—we'll do it harder and with even greater gusto in an anxious emotional field. That's just normal. The important question is, What happens after that? Reactivity . . . and then what?

In some circumstances, we may be able to stand back a bit, tone down our reactivity to the other person, and do some problem solving. We can begin to identify our individual coping style, observe how it interacts with the style of others, and modify our part in stuck patterns that block intimacy. Sometimes, however, we cannot tone down our reactivity by an act of will. We need instead to address the source of anxiety that is revving us up. Frequently, our reactivity in one relationship is fueled by anxiety from an entirely different source. Let's take a look at how such a process can work.

Anxiety and the Pursuit Cycle

A couple of years back, my sister shared with me that she was having a terribly difficult time with her steady companion, David. Although Susan felt entirely committed to the relationship, David said he needed more time to work through his own issues in order to make a decision about living together. This was a difficult situation because Susan and David lived in two different cities, making for long and tiring weekend trips. However, this long-distance arrangement (and David's indecision) was nothing new and had been going on for quite some time.

What *was* new was my sister's sudden feeling of panic, resulting in her pressuring David for a decision he was not ready to make. Because my sister had been working for some time on her pattern of pursuing men who were distancers in romantic relationships, she was able to see her behavior like a red warning flag. She was unable, however, to tone down her reactivity and stop pursuing. By the time Susan called me, she was feeling terrible.

In thinking about my sister's situation, I was particularly struck by the *timing* of the problem. Susan's sense of desperation and her heightened reactivity to David's wish for more time and space followed a trip we took to Phoenix to visit our parents and to see our Uncle Si, who was dying from a fast-moving lung cancer. Si's diagnosis was a shock to us, for he was a vibrant, strapping man we had assumed would outlive everyone. Visiting with him was also a reminder of past losses, impending losses, and some recent health scares and downhill slides in our family tree. Of all of these stressors, the closest to home for Susan and me was an earlier diagnosis that our father had a rare, degenerative brain disease. Because my father surprised everyone by regaining considerable functioning, this devastating diagnosis was replaced with a more hopeful one.

During our phone conversation, I asked Susan if there might be a connection between her anxious focus on David, and all the emotions that were stirred up by our recent visit to Phoenix. This made intellectual sense to her, on the one hand, but on the other, it seemed a bit abstract since Susan was not experiencing a connection at a gut level. Indeed, any of us may have difficulty appreciating that key events in our first family—and how we respond to them—profoundly affect our current (or future) romantic relationships.

Soon thereafter, Susan came to Topeka for a long weekend and decided to consult with a family systems therapist during her visit. As a result, she began to more fully appreciate the link between recent health issues in our family and her anxious pursuit of David. Simply *thinking* about this connection helped Susan to de-intensify her focus on David and reflect more calmly and objectively on her current situation.

Susan was also challenged to think about the pursuer-distancer pattern she was stuck in. It was *as if* 100 percent of the anxiety and ambivalence about living together were David's. It was *as if* Susan were just 100 percent raring to go—no worries at all, she said, except how they would decorate the apartment. Such polarities (she stands for togetherness, he for distance) are common enough, but they distort the experience of self and other, and just keep us stuck.

Finally, Susan confronted the fact that she was putting so much energy into her relationship with David that she was neglecting her own work and failing to pay attention to her short- and long-term career goals. On the one hand, Susan's attention to this relationship made sense because ensuring its success was her highest priority. On the other hand, *focusing on a relationship at the expense of one's own goals and life plan overloads that relationship.* The best way Susan could work on her relationship with David was to work on her own self. This kind of self-focus is a good rule of thumb for all of us.

Having a Plan

Insight and understanding are necessary but insufficient pieces of solving a problem. The next challenge for Susan was translating what she had learned into action. What might Susan do differently upon her return home to lower her anxiety and achieve a calmer, more balanced relationship with David? By the time Susan left Topeka, she had formulated a plan. Whenever we are feeling very anxious, it can be enormously helpful to have a clear plan, a plan based not on reactivity and a reflexive need to "do something" (anything!), but rather on reflection and a solid understanding of our problem.

Breaking the Pursuit Cycle

This is what Susan did differently upon her return home. First, Susan shared with David that she had been thinking about their relationship during their time apart and had gained some insight into her own behavior. "I came to realize," she told David, "that the pressure I was feeling about our living together had less to do with you and our relationship, and more to do with my anxiety about some other things." She filled David in on what these other things were—family issues related to health and loss. David was understanding—and visibly relieved.

Susan also told David that perhaps she was letting him express the ambivalence for *both* of them, which probably wasn't fair. She reminded David that her own track record with relationships surely provided her with good reason to be anxious about commitment, but that she could avoid this pretty well by focusing on *his* problem and *his* wish to put off the decision.

This piece of dialogue was hardest for Susan, because when we are in a pursuer-distancer polarity, the pursuer is convinced that *all* she wants is more togetherness and the distancer is convinced that *all* he wants is more distance. Sometimes only after the pursuit cycle is broken can each party begin to experience the wish for both separateness and togetherness that we all struggle with.

Finally, Susan told David that she had been neglecting her own work projects and needed to put more time and attention into them. "Instead of driving up next weekend," Susan said, "I'm going to stay at home and get some work done." For the first time in a while, Susan became the spokesperson for more distance, *not in an angry, reactive manner but rather as a calm move for self.* Indeed, when Susan began to pay more attention to her work, she became quite anxious about how she had neglected it.

The changes Susan made were effective in breaking the pursuer-distancer pattern that was bringing her pain. If we are pursuers, such moves can be excruciatingly difficult to initiate and sustain in a calm, non-reactive fashion. Pursuing is often a reflexive reaction to anxiety. If it is *our* way, we will initially become *more* anxious when we keep it in check.

From where, then, do we get the motivation and the courage to maintain such a change? As one colleague of mine explains, we get it from the conviction that the old ways simply do not work.

Moving Back to the Source

Before Susan left Topeka, she considered another option aimed at helping her to calm things down with David. Whenever Susan found herself feeling anxious about the relationship and slipping back into the pursuit mode, she would contemplate *sitting down and writing a letter to our*

father instead, or calling home. This may sound a bit farfetched
at first, but it makes good sense. If Susan managed her
anxiety about family issues by distancing, then she would
keep her anxiety down in that arena but she would be more
likely to get intense with David. If she could stay connected
to the *actual source of her anxiety,* then she might become
more anxious about our parent's failing health, for example,
but the anxiety would be less likely to overload her relationship with David. Indeed, learning how to stay in touch with
people on our own family tree, and working on key emotional issues at their source, lays the groundwork for more
solid intimate relationships in the present or future.   ;

Of course, staying connected to family members and
working on these relationships is a challenge requiring considerable time and effort. Indeed, this work really has no end
but by the limits of our own motivation. Had Susan been in
therapy, she might have chosen to continue and deepen this
work over time. But a small step can go a long way. For
Susan, just keeping in touch with family helped to lower her
reactivity to David's caution and occasional distance. And
lowering her reactivity was the key element that allowed
Susan to stay on course in modifying her reflexive pattern of
pursuit.

A Postscript on Partners
Who Can't Make Up Their Minds

What if *your* partner can't make a commitment? What if he's
not ready to think about marriage, not ready to give up
another relationship, not sure that he is really in love? He (or
she) may or may not be ready in two years—or twenty. Does
Susan's story imply that we should hang around forever,

working on our own issues and failing to address our partner's uncertainty? Does it mean that we should never take a position about our partner's distancing or lack of commitment? Certainly not! A partner's long-term ambivalence *is* an issue for us—that is, if we really want to settle down.

We will, however, be *least successful* in addressing the commitment issue—or any issue, for that matter—if we are coming from a reactive and intense place. Working to keep anxiety down is a priority, because anxiety drives reactivity, which drives polarities. (*All* he can do is distance. *All* she can do is pursue.) Of course, anxiety is not something we can eliminate from our lives. Our intimate relationships will always be overloaded with old emotional baggage from our first family as well as recent stresses that hit us from all quarters. But the more we pay attention to the multiple sources of anxiety that impinge on our lives, the more calmly and clearly we'll navigate the hot spots with our intimate other.

A Calm Bottom Line

Let's look at a woman who was able to take a clear position with her distant and ambivalent partner, a position that was relatively free from reactivity and expressions of anxious pursuit. Gwenna was a twenty-six-year-old real estate agent who sought my help about a particular relationship issue. For two and a half years she had been dating Greg, a city planner who had had disastrous first and second marriages and couldn't make up his mind about a third. Gwenna was aware that Greg backed off further under pressure, yet she didn't want to live forever with the status quo. How did she ultimately handle the situation?

As a first step, Gwenna talked with Greg about their relationship, calmly initiating the conversation in a low-keyed fashion. She shared her perspective on both the strengths and weaknesses of their relationship and what her hopes were for their future. She asked Greg to do the same. Unlike earlier conversations, this one was conducted without her pursuing him, pressuring him, or diagnosing his problems with women. At the same time, she asked Greg some clear questions, which exposed his own vagueness.

"How will you know when you *are* ready to make a commitment? What specifically would need to change or be different than it is today?"

"I don't know," was Greg's response. When questioned further, the best he could come up with was that he'd "just feel it."

"How much more time do you need to make a decision one way or another?"

"I'm not sure," Greg replied. "Maybe a couple of years, but I really can't answer a question like that. I can't predict or plan my feelings."

And so it went.

Gwenna really loved this man, but two years (and maybe longer) was longer than she could comfortably wait. So, after much thought, she told Greg that she would wait till fall (about ten months), but that she would move on if he couldn't commit himself to marriage by then. She was open about her own wish to marry and have a family with him, but she was equally clear that her first priority was a mutually committed relationship. If Greg was not at that point by fall, then she would end the relationship—painful though it would be.

During the waiting period, Gwenna was able to *not* pursue him and *not* get distant or otherwise reactive to his expressions of ambivalence and doubt. *In this way she gave Greg emotional space to struggle with his dilemma and the relationship had its best chance of succeeding.* Her bottom-line position ("a decision by fall") was not a threat or an attempt to rope Greg in, but rather a true definition of self and a clarification of the limits of what she could accept and still feel OK about in the relationship and her own self.

Gwenna would not have been able to proceed this way if the relationship was overloaded with baggage from her past and present that she was not paying attention to. During the waiting period, Gwenna put her emotional energy into working on her own issues, which included, among other things, her anger at her deceased father, who she felt had been unavailable to her, and her related pattern of choosing distant males with poor track records in relationships. Of course, hard work does not ensure that things turn out as we wish. While my sister and David now live happily together, Gwenna's story has a different ending.

When fall arrived, Greg told Gwenna he needed another six months to make up his mind. Gwenna deliberated a while and decided she could live with that. But when the six months were up, Greg was still uncertain and asked for more time. It was then that Gwenna took the painful but ultimately empowering step of ending their relationship.

Anxiety . . . From Where and When?

Anxiety. We all know it impacts on everything from our immune system to our closest relationships. How can we identify the significant sources of anxiety and emotional intensity in our lives?

Sometimes they are obvious. There may be a recent stressful event, a negative or even positive change we can pinpoint as a source of anxiety that is overloading a relationship. If *we* miss it, others may see it for us ("No wonder you've been fighting more with Jim—you moved to a new city just a year ago and that's a major adjustment!").

Sometimes we sort of know a particular event or change is stressful, but we don't fully appreciate just *how* stressful it really is. For example, we may downplay the emotional impact of significant transitions—a birth, a child leaving home, a graduation, a wedding, a job change, a promotion, a retirement, or an ill parent—because these are "just normal things" that happen in the course of the life cycle. Other people may even appear to breeze through. We fail to appreciate that "just normal things," when they involve change, will profoundly effect our closest ties.

In other cases we may simply *not* link anxiety from source A to stuckness in relationship B, or we may minimize or ignore the key events in our first family that raise intensity elsewhere. My sister, for example, was initially unaware that her reactive position with David was driven by the emotionality from her family visit, although one followed right on the heels of the other. Our narrow focus on one intimate relationship obscures the broader emotional field from our view.

A Look at the Emotional Field

Consider Heather, who found herself suddenly "swept away" by a married man named Ira and vulnerable to extreme highs and lows in response to Ira's alternating hot and cold attitude toward her. She felt so buffeted about by the intensity of her feelings that she called me to begin psychotherapy.

According to Heather's report, "nothing else was happening" in her life at the time her relationship with Ira heated up. That is, she believed that the beginning of their affair had occurred in a calm emotional field. When I inquired carefully, however, I learned that Heather's passionate attachment to Ira began shortly after the death of her maternal grandmother. Because this grandmother was a distant figure in Heather's life, this loss did not seem to Heather to be of particular emotional significance.

But such was not the case. Heather's widowed mother and grandmother had been extremely close, spending much of their time together. The grandmother's death raised uncomfortable issues for Heather concerning her mother's well-being and also evoked Heather's worry that she was next in line to fill up the empty space in her mother's life. It also stirred up strong feelings about the earlier loss of her own dad. As Heather was to learn, our distance from family members is by no means a protection from strong emotional reactions to their deaths.

The underground emotionality surrounding her grandmother's death created an anxious emotional field in which Heather's painful attachment to Ira took hold. Her reactivity to Ira's every move was sky-high. Yet from Heather's perspective, "nothing else was happening" when their steamy affair began.

Sometimes the source of anxiety or intensity that is fueling a current relationship problem is from an experience long past—incest, an early loss, or any number of "hot issues" in our first family which were never processed or resolved. The trauma, or the problem in the family that could not be talked about, might be from five years ago or fifty-five. The connection may be relatively easy to make ("I know that my problem with being intimate with Sam has something to do with my history of sexual abuse"). Or we may be unable to make a connection at all.

Consider, for example, Lois and Frances, two sisters in their late forties who barely speak to each other since their mother's death six years ago. Lois is still furious at Frances for not doing enough for their mother at the time of her greatest need, and Frances believes Lois made unilateral decisions about their mother's care without consulting her. The two sisters are locked in a mutually blaming stance, heading for a total cutoff that will likely continue in successive generations. Each considers "the problem" to be the fault of the other. Neither sister is aware that the intensity in their relationship (managed first by fighting and now by distance) has as its source the high level of anxiety surrounding their mother's terminal illness and death.

Staying angry and distant protects both Lois and Frances from the full experience of their grief, which they would meet head on if they truly reconciled and drew together. It also protects Lois from experiencing her anger *at her mother,* who left Frances more than half of the inheritance because Lois had a wealthier husband. Their stuck position blocks them from successfully mourning the loss of their mother, processing the issue of the inheritance, and affirming their important bond as sisters.

Six years after losing their mother, Lois and Frances have not yet moved out of their reactive way of relating to each other. Perhaps at some future time a crisis, or some other transforming life experience, will allow one of them to take the first bold move toward connectedness. If this occurs, it will surely constitute a courageous act of change.

Thinking About Anniversaries

Our closest relationships are like lightning rods that absorb tensions and anxieties from whatever source and from however long ago. *Anniversary dates will always kick up anxiety, whether we are aware of them or not.* For me, hitting my forties presents a challenge because my mother was diagnosed with her first cancer in her late forties—and her mother died at age forty-four. I trust the fifties will be easier, all other things being equal, which of course they never are. If a crisis hit your family when you were age six, you can be certain that you'll be operating in a more anxious emotional field when your child turns six and when you reach the age your mother was at that time.

This does not mean we will *feel* more anxious at an important anniversary date. When your daughter reaches age nine, the age you were when your parents divorced, you may not even remember that fact. Instead you may feel more critical of your husband, or perhaps feel more clingy and insecure. Or instead you may find that you and your daughter become quite distant—or that you fight with her daily about her school habits or choice of friends.

What we see most frequently at anniversary dates is the *outcome* of high anxiety, those predictable patterned ways in which people move under stress that rigidify and polarize our relationships. Some people *do* make the connection ("I notice I've wanted to leave Joe since I've been approaching the age of my mother's breakdown"). Most of us don't. Instead we just shift into a reactive gear and a particular relationship may take a downward spiraling turn. Or we just get reactive all over the place. Our boss criticizes our work and a cloud of depression settles over us all day. A boyfriend seeks more space and we feel panicky. We're just more vulnerable to automatic, intense reactions from whatever source.

Of course, none of this is exactly new. We all know there are multiple sources of stress that impact on a particular relationship at a particular time. And of course we are aware that anxieties and unresolved issues from our first family get us into trouble today. *Thinking* about key sources of anxiety, however, is a big challenge. *Working* on them is a bigger one still.

What Is the Problem?

Most of us confuse the *outcome* of high anxiety with "the problem." For example, I was viewed as "the problem" at the time of my mother's cancer diagnosis and I was sent to therapy. It would have been just as likely for anxiety to be managed by severe marital fighting or distance, in which case a "marital problem" might have been the diagnosis. In another family, Dad might have hit the bottle or Mother might have developed a severe depression with other family members getting organized around it in an unhelpful fashion.

When anxiety overloads a family beyond their resources to manage it, they will come to therapy naming the problem in one of three ways:

1. *Child-focus:* A child is seen as the problem and everything else may be viewed as OK.
2. *Marital fighting and/or distance:* "The marriage" is the problem.
3. *A symptomatic spouse:* One spouse is underfunctioning or has the symptom.

When *one* person or *one* relationship is labeled "the problem," other issues get obscured from view. For example, if my sister saw David's distancing (or her own pursuing) as "the real problem," she would have missed the point. On the one hand, it was helpful for her to observe and modify her own part in a pattern of distance and pursuit that was only bringing her pain. In that sense, the *pattern* was the problem. On the other hand, it was equally important that she widen her focus to include additional sources of anxiety that were fueling her reactivity.

Maintaining a broad perspective isn't easy. Naturally we want to focus where it hurts and we want to steer clear of other areas. For example, if we bring our child to therapy, we want the focus of treatment to be on the child. Our concern for our child is genuine enough. However, the *last thing* we want is to look at our own reactivity toward the child's father or stepmother, or how we are currently navigating our own relationship with our mother.

We want to look where we want to look. And the higher the anxiety, the more extreme our tunnel vision and the greater our vulnerability to be swallowed up by painful feelings. Yet, as the next chapter continues to illustrate, we cannot work on intimacy problems if we stay narrowly focused on one relationship or on any one definition of "the problem."

5

Distance and More Distance

Adrienne called me for an appointment with the goal of working on her marriage. She summarized the problem in these words: "Frank and I got along fine for the first few years. But after our second child was born, we began to fight a lot. And when we both had enough of that, we just stopped relating to each other and became like roommates sharing an apartment. I was devastated when I discovered he was having an affair, but I shouldn't have been surprised. I was looking at another man, too, even though I wasn't acting on it."

If not for the painful discovery of her husband's lover, Adrienne might not have come for help. "I knew the closeness had gone out of our relationship, both physically and emotionally," she explained, "but I wasn't that upset about it. Maybe I was denying the problem, but I figured it was just life. A lot of couples I know aren't intimate after they have kids. Every now and then the distance really bothered me, but at the same time I didn't take it that seriously. I suppose I got used to it."

When Adrienne first sought my help, she viewed distance as the problem in her marriage. Earlier, she had viewed marital fighting as the problem. Distancing and fighting, however, are not "the problem" between any two people. Both conflict and distance are normal ways of managing the anxiety that is freighting an important relationship.

Given sufficient time and the inevitable stresses that the life cycle brings, we can count on periods of reactive fighting and distance in even the most ideal partnerships. The fight-or-flight response is present in all species, our own included. The *degree* of trouble we get into in a particular relationship rests on two factors. The first is the amount of stress and anxiety that is impinging on a relationship from multiple sources, past and present. The second is the *amount of self* that we bring to that relationship. To the extent that we have not carved out a clear and whole "I" in our first family, we will always feel in some danger of being swallowed up by the "togetherness force" with others. Seeking distance (or fighting) is an almost instinctual reaction to the anxiety over this *fusion,* this togetherness which threatens loss of self.

The specific *way* we get into trouble has to do with our own particular style of managing anxiety and the dances we get stuck in with others. Adrienne's story will allow us to take an in-depth look at one common, if not universal, way of managing anxiety that can get us in trouble over the long haul in any close relationship: *emotional distance and cutoff.*

Distancing: The Problem or the Solution?

What is a distant relationship? Adrienne's description of her marriage to Frank provides a good example. At the time she discovered her husband's affair, they seldom fought, but at the same time they were not really close and they rarely shared their thoughts, feelings, and experiences. And rather than confront the distance in their relationship head-on, both of them were detouring their emotional energy toward a third party. Frank was having an affair, and although Adrienne was not sleeping with anyone, she had another man under her skin.

In one sense, Frank's affair—and Adrienne's affair of the mind—protected their marriage. Adrienne's erotic attachment to another man ensured that she would not fully experience her dissatisfaction with Frank, and thus the deeper problems in her marriage would not surface with real emotional force. When we look later at the complex business of triangles, we will see how third parties *do* serve to stabilize relationships and help keep the real issues safely underground. Of course, the solution is also the problem. Adrienne and Frank became so entrenched in an empty-shell relationship that it took a real crisis—Adrienne's discovery of the "other woman"—to get her to take a serious look at their marriage, and her life.

Most of us rely on some form of distancing as a primary way to manage intensity in key relationships, including those in our first family. For example, we may move to a different city or country as a way to avoid the difficult feelings evoked by closer contact with our parents or other family members. Or we may live in our folks' house but withdraw emotionally by keeping conversations superficial, by sharing little about our selves, or by avoiding certain subjects entirely. We may even have a sibling we don't speak to unless we happen to show up together at a family gathering.

Emotional distancing can be an essential first move to ensure our emotional well-being and even our survival. We all know from personal experience that a relationship can become so emotionally charged that the most productive action we can take is to seek space. And if we are in danger of violence or abuse, there is no higher priority than getting out of the situation to ensure that we will not be hurt.

Distancing is a useful way to manage intensity when it removes us from a situation of high reactivity and allows us to get calm enough to reflect, plan, and generate new options for our behavior. Often, however, we rely on distance and a cutoff to exit permanently (emotionally or physically) from a significant relationship, without really addressing the issues and problems. This may be the easiest and least painful way out in the short run—but whatever goes unresolved and unprocessed may cause trouble in our next relationship venture. As usual, it's a matter of short-term relief in exchange for a long-term cost.

In Adrienne's marriage the distance was extreme. At the same time, however, the triangles (Frank's affair and Adrienne's serious flirtation) stabilized the marriage so that neither partner was pushing for change—that is, not until the cat got out of the bag and there was no way to put it back in.

Back to the Emotional Field

All of us, without exception, have difficulty with intimacy, and over time, we will either move forward or drift backward in this dimension. Why did Adrienne move backward, and why did the distance in her marriage become so extreme?

According to Adrienne, marital problems "just happened" after the birth of Joe, their second son. But conflict in relationships does not "just happen," nor do people simply, without reason, drift into intractable fighting or distance. What, then, was the broader context for Adrienne and Frank's relationship difficulties? What was going on at around the time that Adrienne and Frank entered a period of constant fighting and bickering, and then one of unbridgeable distance, lack of communication, and infidelity? "Nothing much," according to Adrienne. On careful investigation, however, "nothing much" turned out to be a great deal, indeed.

Although Adrienne herself observed that marital tensions surfaced after the birth of Joe, their second son, she failed to associate the two events. Yet the connection was real enough. The birth of any child introduces extra stress into a marriage, and for this couple, the issue of second sons was a particularly loaded one. *What made it loaded was the history of "second sons" in the previous generation in each of their own families.*

In Adrienne's family, the second child, Greg, was born severely retarded and was placed in an institution when he was three. When I began seeing Adrienne in psychotherapy, she had not visited her younger brother for eleven years, because "he doesn't recognize anyone and there's no point." In Frank's family, the second and youngest son had been the "problem child," who was still considered something of a black sheep. Given these emotional issues surrounding second sons, it was no surprise that Joe's entrance into the family would evoke a fair share of underground anxiety and concern.

During Joe's first year of life, Adrienne's father was diagnosed with stomach cancer that was discovered at an advanced stage. Although Adrienne was terribly upset about her dad's diagnosis, she managed her feelings by distancing from him. She did not decrease the *amount* of contact she had with her father, but all her communication about his illness and her reactions to it were through her mother, who took the position that Adrienne's father needed to be protected from what was happening. When I first met with Adrienne, her father was at the terminal stage of his illness, but she had not yet found a way to even mention the cancer to him, to say good-bye, or to tell him how much she valued him as her father.

At the time that her marital problems intensified, Adrienne was also struggling with career issues. When Joe was born, Frank had managed his own anxiety by distancing into long hours of overtime work. On the surface, Adrienne fought with him about his unavailability, but she was also envious of his ability to lose himself in his projects. In contrast, she was experiencing increasing dissatisfaction with her own job as a lab technician but was unable to generate alternatives or to clarify what she wanted to do. By entering into a strong, erotic flirtation with a man at work, Adrienne put her own career issues on hold and helped to steady the marital boat—while she and Frank grew oceans apart.

It was an important first step for Adrienne to recognize the high stress she had been under since the birth of her second son, and to more clearly identify the key events that helped fuel the growing distance in her marriage. These were:

- the birth of a new baby, Joe, which evoked deep (although unconscious) feelings in Adrienne about her own retarded brother and his place in the family.
- the diagnosis of her father's terminal illness.

- Adrienne's own career concerns and her difficulty formulating personal goals.

It was also reassuring for Adrienne to recognize that when anxiety and stress get high enough, or last long enough, marital distancing and/or fighting is one common way that it gets expressed.

From Insight to Action

As Adrienne looked carefully and objectively at how she negotiated other important relationships under stress, she began to observe that distancing was a long-standing pattern for her and other members of her family. It was, in fact, her familiar and preferred way of moving under stress, especially with men. In her first family, her relationship with two important males—her dad and her retarded brother—had always been distant, with her mother in the middle, conveying information between parties. Through therapy, Adrienne began to recognize that there was some connection between her distant position from the men in her first family and the dramatic distance that now characterized her marriage.

Wouldn't it be nice if "insight" automatically led to change? Typically it does not. Understanding the roots of a problem is not the same as knowing how to solve it.

As Adrienne learned more about herself in psychotherapy, she tried to move back into her marriage in a new way, hoping to achieve a deeper level of closeness. Some of what she did differently was ultimately productive. For example, she told Frank that psychotherapy was helping her to become aware of her *own* contribution to the distance in their marriage, which she was working to change. She also took a clear position that his extramarital affair was not acceptable to her and that he would have to end it in order for her to stay in the marriage. This he did.

But much of Adrienne's efforts to "push closeness" only interfered with its attainment. She became preoccupied with intimacy as a primary goal, keeping it in the forefront of her discussions with Frank and insisting that he join with her in the pursuit of it. The more she pursued Frank for greater closeness, and the more she focused on his lack of warmth, interest, and attentiveness, the more distant Frank became. And the more he distanced, the more Adrienne pursued.

What happened when Adrienne was able to break the pursuit-distance cycle? She accomplished this by de-intensifying her critical focus on Frank and by giving him more space, without returning to her earlier position of cold withdrawal. In response, Frank did make some tentative moves toward her. At this point, however, Adrienne responded negatively—she just wanted to be left alone. "To be really honest," she reflected in psychotherapy, "maybe it's too late. Or maybe I really don't want to be particularly close with him. But I don't want to lose the marriage."

Adrienne gradually recognized her own allergy to intimacy, which helped her to realize that she needed to make changes in her original family relationships before she could move differently in her marriage. This gave Adrienne the courage to go "back home" again. If she chose to remain cutoff from the males in her first family and failed to process emotional issues in that arena, then her marriage would remain overloaded. And Adrienne would continue to respond to the overload by distancing or with conflict.

"Dad, I'm Going to Miss You"

How did Adrienne move against the distance in her own family? First, she made a significant effort to connect with her dad directly about his illness rather than hearing all the details via her mom. The typical pattern was that Adrienne always began her visits with her dad by asking, "How are you?"—to which he responded with a superficial reply ("About the same") or with a somewhat loaded joke ("The doctors tell me I'm so healthy I could drop dead any minute"). Adrienne would then change the subject and they would chat about the weather or the grandchildren.

Adrienne made a big advance when she was able to cut through her father's distance (which was his attempt to offer Adrienne the protection *he* thought *she* needed) and ask him directly, "Dad, what are the doctors telling you about your cancer? I'd really like to hear the facts from you." When he gave his usual superficial and uninformative response, she let him know directly that although his cancer—and her awareness that she might lose him soon—was painful for her, she would feel much better if she knew the facts and was kept informed. When he said, "Mother will keep you informed," Adrienne responded, "She does, Dad, but I'd also like to hear it from you." This brief conversation was a big step for Adrienne in dealing more directly with her dad's impending death. It was also the first time that the word "cancer" had been used by any family member in her father's presence. He reacted awkwardly at first and then later with relief and greater openness.

Of course, there were times when Adrienne's dad did not feel like talking about his illness, and Adrienne was sensitive to his moods. It is of questionable virtue to push someone into discussing something because *we* think it is good to do so. But often we confuse sensitivity with an anxious "protectiveness" in which the lines of communication shut down in a family because everyone operates on the assumption that the *other* person doesn't want to hear it or can't handle it.

Initially, Adrienne was convinced that her father chose not to discuss his own dying ("He can't deal with it") and that bringing it up was intrusive. This notion was reinforced by her mother, who insisted that Adrienne's father "could never deal with reality." *Yet Adrienne herself was not asking her father questions that made clear her wish to keep the lines of communication open.* Adrienne made a courageous change in her own relationship with her dad when she began to calmly and clearly ask questions.

What sorts of questions? Adrienne's questions conveyed her interest in the facts of his illness as the doctors saw it ("Did you get the results of the test back?" "What is your doctor telling you about your prognosis and the course of the cancer?"). Her questions conveyed her interest in her dad's own perspective ("Do you agree with the doctors or see it differently?" "What's your own sense about this cancer and your prognosis?") And her questions conveyed her interest in her dad's thoughts and feelings about death.

When, through her questions and the sharing of her own reactions, Adrienne convinced her father of *her* genuine wish to know, he turned out to value the opportunity to talk about his terminal condition. A week before he died, Adrienne's father shared his "philosophy of death" with her and they did some crying together. Later that week Adrienne told me, "It was a good kind of crying—not a depressed crying, but just an emotional crying."

As Adrienne put her emotional energy into connecting with her family around her father's impending death, she experienced great sadness but also felt as if a load had lifted from her marriage. She became less preoccupied with "lack of intimacy" as a root difficulty in her marriage, and paradoxically, she became better able to achieve it. As her marriage became freer from the emotional overload of an important mourning process, Adrienne also became freer to share with Frank what she was going through as her dad was dying. She was able to focus more on how *she* was managing her own issues, and less on whether Frank was responding to her self-disclosures in just the "right way." As a result, she and Frank shared more instances of genuine closeness.

"My Brother Means Nothing to Me"

The most distant relationship in Adrienne's life was with her brother. She treated it as a "non-relationship" and did her best to render Greg invisible in her mind. It is not possible, however, to have a "non-relationship" with a parent or sibling. Distance and cutoff only cause intensity to go underground and resurface elsewhere.

For a long time in psychotherapy, Adrienne could not *think* about her brother, Greg, much less contemplate a visit to the institution where he resided. Each time I asked a simple factual question about Greg, or inquired about how his retardation and institutionalization affected the family, Adrienne gave the same predictable response: "I never knew him—he's too retarded to relate to—he means nothing to me."

Adrienne had not seen Greg for over a decade, and prior to that her contact with him had been minimal. His status as an "invisible" family member was more than apparent. Adrienne's older son, who was five, did not even know that his mother had a brother. Frank had never met Greg or seen a photograph of him as an adult. Adrienne herself might not have recognized Greg if she had run into him on the street.

Adrienne talked about her lifelong distance from Greg as if it reflected nothing more than disinterest ("I simply can't think of any reason why I'd go to the trouble to see him"). She was totally unaware of the underground feelings that threatened to surface if she made any move to reconnect. "This may sound callous," she would report blandly, "but I just don't consider him a member of the family."

We commonly confuse distance or cutoff with a defect of the heart. We hear this confusion in everyday talk, and even in the pronouncements of mental health experts. Labels like "unloving" or "uncaring" may automatically be applied to a mother who relinquishes or takes flight from her child, to a father who abandons the family and never looks back, to a brother who cuts off communication with his sister after she enters a psychiatric hospital or becomes ill.

It is important to understand that distance and cutoff between family members have nothing to do with an absence of feeling, or a lack of love or concern. Distance and cutoff are simply ways of managing anxiety. Rather than reflecting a *lack* of feeling, they reflect an *intensity* of feeling. The feeling may surround hot issues that have evolved over many generations and that cannot be processed or even mentioned easily.

Adrienne learned the true meaning of intensity only *after* she telephoned the institution where her brother lived and set up a date for the long trip to a neighboring state to see him. The week before the visit, she was unable to sleep well, had terrifying and violent nightmares, and experienced her first full-blown panic attack on the bus to work one day.

For reasons she could not articulate, she felt unable to tell her mom about the visit, so kept it a secret.

These dramatic reactions to Adrienne's planned visit forced her to recognize that seeing her brother was no small emotional matter. Still, it was only *after* she visited Greg that she could begin to identify and process the underground feelings that the distance and cutoff had held in check.

Fallout from Change

After so much anticipatory anxiety, Adrienne found the actual visit to Greg reassuring. Their meeting stayed on a calm note, and although Adrienne was convinced that her status as a sister went unappreciated, Greg seemed pleased by her presence. Having the chance to actually see Greg, to be with him, to observe the setting he was in, and to meet a few staff members who had daily contact with him made Greg into a "real person" for her, and allowed her to replace fantasy with a more realistic perspective on her brother. What made the deepest impression on Adrienne, though, was that one young staff member at the institution was obviously fond of Greg, a feeling he apparently reciprocated. "It never occurred to me that anyone could actually become *attached* to him—or vice versa!" Adrienne exclaimed during her next therapy session. "I mean this guy seemed to have a real affection for Greg, like they had a *real relationship.*"

Because Adrienne initially found the visit reassuring, she was unprepared for its emotional aftermath. Several weeks after she shared the news of her visit to Greg with her mom, Adrienne came to therapy nearly hysterical. Her mother, Elaine, was acutely depressed and had shared suicidal fantasies with her, although she had no plan to act on them. The following week, I saw Adrienne and her mother together.

Over the next several sessions with Adrienne and Elaine, a crucial family theme erupted—a theme that had seethed like an underground volcano since Greg's birth. This "hot issue" was Greg's retardation and, more specifically, the unspoken question in the family of "Who was to blame?" What emerged through Elaine's outpouring of tears and despair was her most profound sense of guilt and self-recrimination for the condition of her son.

Adrienne's cutoff from her brother had helped protect her mother from the conscious recognition of these feelings, and protected the family from having to deal with a subject that everyone feared was too hot to handle. At an unconscious level, Adrienne had always appreciated this fact. Children usually do.

During our time together, Adrienne's mother was able to share with her daughter the questions about her son's retardation that had haunted her for decades. Had she caused it? Was it a gene from her side of the family? Was it the bottle of wine she had drunk during that first month when she didn't know she was pregnant? Elaine also shared her profound guilt about the decision to institutionalize Greg. She told Adrienne, in a voice filled more with despair than blame, "When you kept talking on and on about how much that man liked Greg—and how they seemed to really be good for each other—I thought you were telling me that I was a monster for putting him away!"

In a way, all this was new to Adrienne. But in a way it was not, for she had always sensed the unnamed tension surrounding the subject of Greg. As Adrienne and her mother were able to share their thoughts and reactions on this difficult subject, her mother's depression rapidly lifted. At the same time, however, a second "hot issue" emerged, as Elaine got in touch with her previously repressed rage at her deceased husband. Elaine had always felt that her husband's family blamed her for the decision to institutionalize Greg, and she believed that her husband had not come to her defense. She and her husband had not talked about this directly, but it provided the backdrop for their own growing marital distance. Indeed, after *their* second child, Greg, Elaine and her husband had drifted into a growing distance, *a pattern that Adrienne could now recognize herself repeating.*

Both Adrienne and Elaine found it awkward and difficult to talk openly about these painful issues, but it was ultimately rewarding. As a result of getting things out on the table, mother and daughter shared a genuinely closer relationship and both were freer to stay in more emotional contact with Greg. Elaine's self-disclosure helped Adrienne to recognize that *she too felt guilty:* guilty because she had never wanted Greg to come along in the first place; guilty because she had wanted him gone from the moment he arrived; guilty because, in the omnipotent unconscious mind of the child, these "bad feelings" had *caused* her brother to be extruded from the family; and finally, guilty because her life was so easy and privileged compared to the hardship that Greg's handicap imposed on him.

When Adrienne could articulate these guilty feelings, think about them, talk about them with family members, and recognize that they were both *natural* and *shared,* her unconscious no longer needed to "do penance" for her sins. Much to Adrienne's surprise, she found herself thinking more creatively about her work situation, as her own guilt about having a retarded brother was no longer a restraining force.

Adrienne's guilt, however, did not derive entirely from early irrational sources. Adrienne also felt guilty because she had rendered her brother invisible and treated him as if he did not exist. *Because women are encouraged to feel guilty about*

*everything—and to take responsibility for all human problems—
we often have difficulty sorting out when guilt is there for a good
reason.* By "good reason" I refer to guilt that lets us know we
are not taking a responsible position in a relationship: *a
position that is congruent with our own values and beliefs as we
have struggled to formulate them, separate from pressures of family
and culture.*

Only *after* visiting her brother and breaking the old distancing pattern did Adrienne become aware of her strong
feelings of guilt for having stayed away. This awareness led to
changed behavior, as it should. Adrienne slowly began to
stay in reasonable contact with her brother, and she brought
her children and husband to meet him as well. Whether Greg
recognized her as family or fully appreciated her visits was
not entirely clear at the time Adrienne terminated her work
with me. Adrienne had nonetheless decided to stay connected—for her own sake.

What About Adrienne's Marriage?

Adrienne came into therapy with only one goal and only one
area of concern: She wanted to save her marriage. She had
no wish to talk about her father's impending death, and the
subject of her retarded brother was even more off-limits. "I
can't stand talking about this family stuff!" she would frequently say to me. "What does it have to do with anything?"

Adrienne's feelings were more than understandable.
Our desire not to focus where it hurts makes sense and
should always be respected. This is where Adrienne and I
began, and we might not have needed to look further. *In most
cases, however, couples cannot achieve greater intimacy by staying
narrowly focused on their relationship.* Because our current

relationship problems are fueled by other unresolved issues and affected by how we understand and navigate family relationships, it just doesn't help to stay locked into a narrow perspective.

As Adrienne was able to identify a long-standing pattern of distancing in her family (a pattern that had gone on for at least several generations) and then was able to connect more directly with her family members, her behavior with Frank gradually shifted. Rather than swinging back and forth between distance, on the one hand, and "pushing" for intimacy, on the other, Adrienne found a new middle ground. She moved from self-defeating attempts to be closer (like blaming Frank for being a distant person and pushing him to reveal himself) to constructive attempts (letting Frank know that she wanted to spend a weekend together in the city; sharing more of herself with him, without focusing on whether she got the "right" response). By dealing directly with issues in her own family of origin, rather than avoiding them, Adrienne gained the ability to think more objectively and calmly about her marital difficulties.

There was another reason why Adrienne could not achieve her goal of "closeness" by staying narrowly fixed on her marriage. Paradoxically, couples become less able to achieve intimacy as they stay focused on it and give it their primary attention. *Real closeness occurs most reliably not when it is pursued or demanded in a relationship, but when both individuals work consistently on their own selves.* By "working on the self," I do not mean that we should maintain a single-minded focus on self-actualization, self-enhancement, or career advancement. These are male-defined notions of selfhood that we would do well to challenge. Working on the self includes clarifying beliefs, values, and life goals, staying responsibly connected to persons on one's own family tree, defining the

"I" in key relationships, and addressing important emotional issues as they arise.

Surely, it was important for Adrienne to take the distance in her marriage seriously. For some time before discovering her husband's affair, she had not taken it seriously enough. And yet, it was equally important for her to let go of her overriding preoccupation with intimacy as a primary goal, in order to be better able to achieve it.

As Adrienne paid attention to her important family relationships she became more self-focused and less reactive to Frank's every move. Lowering our reactivity is always a challenge and a prerequisite for working on relationship issues in a productive way. Not surprisingly, the challenge is particularly difficult when that other person is pushing our buttons by not thinking, feeling, and reacting as we do—or as we think they should.

6

Dealing with Differences

"My brother's views on divorce drive me crazy!"

"I simply can't accept the fact that my sister doesn't visit Dad at the hospital."

"It infuriates me that my best friend refuses to join AA when she needs it so desperately!"

"Why doesn't he talk *about things when he's upset!"*

It's hard to feel intimate with someone we disagree with. Surely relationships would be calmer and simpler if everyone thought, felt, and reacted exactly as we do. Believing that one view of reality (usually our own) is the correct one, that different ways of thinking or being in the world mean that one person is "right" and the other is "wrong," is just human nature. We commonly confuse *closeness* with *sameness* and view intimacy as the merging of two separate "I's" into one worldview.

Some differences are bound to make us feel angry, isolated, and anxious at times—and for this reason it may be
hard to keep in mind that *differences are the only way we learn.*
If our world—or even our intimate relationships—were
comprised only of people identical to ourselves, our personal growth would come to an abrupt halt.

But perhaps more to the point is the fact that people *are*
different. *All of us see the world through a different filter, creating as many views of reality as there are people in it.* We view the
world through the unique filter of our age, race, gender,
ethnic background, religion, sibling position, and social
class, for starters. And our particular view of a "correct"
reality will be further refined by our family history, a history
which has evolved particular myths, party lines, and traditions over many generations, along with particular require-
ments for sameness and for change. This is an easy point to
"get" intellectually but not emotionally. Until we can truly
appreciate and respect this concept of *a different filter,* we are
bound to lose perspective. It will require just a little bit of
stress to get us overfocused on what the other party is doing
wrong—or not doing right—and underfocused on the self.

This is not to deny our strong human need to connect
with people like ourselves. Certainly we feel a special closeness to others who share our deeply held beliefs and values,
who enjoy similar interests and activities, and who do things
our way. But in any close relationship differences will inevitably emerge—differences in values, beliefs, priorities, and
habits, *as well as differences in how we manage anxiety and
navigate relationships under stress.*

When anxiety lasts long enough, these differences may
calcify into exaggerated positions in a relationship, as they
did in my own family during my mother's illness. And if we

react strongly to differences (distancing or focusing on the other in an intense way), things may go from bad to worse.

The examples I am about to share with you illustrate the challenge we face in accepting differences and becoming less reactive to that other person who is pushing our buttons or not doing things our way. We will see that this can be a relatively manageable challenge in some circumstances and feel virtually impossible in others.

Dealing with Differences

Suzanne was an anthropologist who had spent several years studying child-rearing patterns in Southeast Asia. She spoke three foreign languages fluently, and by virtue of both her training and personal bent, she was deeply interested in people of other cultures.

Learning to be a calm, nonjudgmental, and objective observer of differences was Suzanne's stock-in-trade. But like the rest of us, this did not generalize to her closest relationships. When Suzanne first came to my office for a consultation, she was furious at her husband, John, for being "tied to his parents' apron strings." John accompanied her to the session, begrudgingly, and only much later returned on his own initiative.

I learned that John, the firstborn and best educated of three sons, was the only sibling to have moved away from the New York area where his Italian grandparents had first settled. Six months ago, his mother had suffered a serious stroke, and John was struggling with guilt feelings about living so far from the family home, leaving his dad and two younger brothers to carry the major burden of day-to-day care. Suzanne felt increasingly unsympathetic to her husband's struggle, which included endless emotional phone calls home. "John has never really separated from his parents," Suzanne explained during our initial meeting, with no attempt to disguise the frustration she was feeling. "My husband is much more tied to *them* than he is to *me!*"

Suzanne had initially requested my help for "marital problems," but it quickly became evident that she viewed John—along with his "sticky, demanding family"—as the problem. Predictably, John was convinced that Suzanne was the problem. She was, by his report, cold and critical, without empathy or appreciation for his dilemma.

A Matter of Ethnicity

Ethnicity is just one of many filters through which we see the world, but since Suzanne was an anthropologist, it seemed like a logical place to help her adopt a more reflective attitude about the differences that concerned her. Suzanne came from an Anglo-Saxon, Protestant background, John from an Italian one. Could Suzanne begin to appreciate these two different "cultures" with the same objectivity, neutrality, and calm with which she contrasted child-rearing practices in America and China? Of course not. But perhaps she could move a bit in this direction. This was the challenge, and a difficult one at that, particularly because Suzanne was operating under the sway of such strong feelings.

What Is a "Family"?

Suzanne knew something about the differing traditions from which she and John came, but she hadn't really given it much thought. When she became curious enough to do some reading on the subject, she explored what was known about how these two ethnic groups think about family and how they define their responsibility to the older generations. The research made her feel right at home.

Italian families place the strongest emphasis on *togetherness*. One does not really think of the individual (the "I") apart from the family, nor of the nuclear family apart from the extended family. The marriage of a child, for example, does not signify the "launching" of that child into the *outside* world, but rather the bringing of a new person *into* the family. With such high value placed on *taking care of one's own*, no one should have to go *outside* the family resources to solve problems or ask for help.

For white Protestants of British origin, the definition of "family" contrasts sharply. For Suzanne's ethnic group, family is a *collection of individuals*, with a few distinguished ancestors that one is not supposed to boast about. A high premium is placed on children leaving home at the appropriate age—launched into the world as separate, self-reliant, and competent individuals.

No wonder Suzanne and John had differing beliefs on such key issues as family loyalty and closeness, and the caretaking of aging parents! As did their families. John's family wanted him home. They were proud of his successes but felt betrayed and puzzled by his move halfway across the country, away from his roots. Suzanne's parents, in contrast, valued the separateness of individual family members. Grown children were expected to be competent and responsible during family crises—but "responsible" did not mean "togetherness," which only made Suzanne's family uncomfortable, particularly at times of stress.

A Warning About Generalizations

Thinking about her marriage in terms of ethnic differences allowed Suzanne to gain a more respectful appreciation of the *different filters* through which we see the world. Generalizations are of course potentially problematic because they can be used to stereotype people rather than to help us recognize the unique screen through which we filter our experience. When we generalize about any group ("The Irish are this way," "Firstborns are that way," "Women are this way") we *exaggerate* similarities within the group and *minimize* similarities between groups. Obviously there is great diversity in any group and countless exceptions to every rule.

When generalizations are made about subordinate group members, we need to be especially wary. Throughout the recorded history of "Mankind," generalizations about women (made in the name of God, nature, and science) have served the interests of the dominant group, defining "separate but equal" spheres which keep women in place and obscure the necessity for social change. As women, over generations, have fit themselves to these prescriptions of what is right and appropriate for our sex, the costs have been incalculable.

Generalizations do not tell us anything about "right" or "wrong," "better" or "worse," "natural" or "God-given." *They are useful only when they foster a greater respect and appreciation for our different constructions of reality that evolve out of different contexts.* In Suzanne's case, for example, her willingness to turn a scholarly eye on the subject of ethnicity helped her to stop *diagnosing* her husband's guilty struggle with conflicting loyalties and begin to see it as a *difference* that was a natural evolution of family patterns and traditions. As she became less reactive to his behaviors and less focused on them, she took the first steps toward changing a stuck marital battle and moved the relationship toward a calmer and more respectful togetherness.

Opposites Attract—and Then What?

Suzanne and John illustrate that old adage "Opposites attract." *Differences* may draw us like a magnet to the other person; however, these *same* differences may repel us later on. What initially attracts us and what later becomes "the problem" are usually one and the same—like the qualities that were most and least valued in my women's group.

John came from a tightly knit family which operated in a "one for all and all for one" fashion. As he increasingly struggled to establish an identity of his own, he became allergic to the high degree of closeness, togetherness, and emotionality in his family. In reaction to this, John was drawn to women who modeled a position of emotional detachment and distance. He fell in love with Suzanne, whose family prized emotional separateness and placed a high premium on the calm self-reliance of individual family members.

Suzanne, for her part, was allergic to the distance and superficiality in her own family. She felt especially drawn to John's large and expressive extended family. But what were her complaints five years into their marriage? Suzanne felt closed in and suffocated by John's "demanding" family ("It's like a big sticky cocoon") and she was mad at John for not "cutting the apron strings." From John's perspective, the "cool and clean" emotional attitude that had first attracted him was now his primary source of dissatisfaction.

Getting Self-Focused

The more Suzanne could think in terms of "cultural differences" between herself and John, the more she could lighten up. And the more Suzanne lightened up, the more effectively John struggled with his own problem. Suzanne didn't really need to become an expert on ethnicity to improve her relationship. Ethnic differences, like birth order, are just one of countless factors that influence our definition of self, our life course, and how we negotiate relationships. For Suzanne, however, her "research" helped her become less negatively focused on John's problem. Her newfound objectivity was a crucial first step toward change.

As Suzanne became less reactive to her husband's struggle, she was able to pay more attention to her own unfinished business with her first family. Suzanne bristled over John's long phone calls home, in part because of her distance from her own family. Slowly, Suzanne began to establish more direct emotional contact with her parents and sister, and in turn she became less focused on what John was or was not doing with his parents and relatives. *When we are not paying enough attention to how we are connecting with our own family, we will be overreactive to our in-laws—or to how our spouse is conducting his family business.*

Although Suzanne learned to stay out of John's family affairs, she did speak up about issues that affected her directly. For example, she and John were planning an eight-day visit to the East Coast; John's family was insisting that he and Suzanne stay with them the entire time. Suzanne, for her part, felt "claustrophobic" about the arrangement and wanted to stay with friends and just visit John's family during the day. Her husband's initial position was that his family would never understand or accept such an arrangement—and that he would not even consider it.

In the old pattern, Suzanne would hover around John during his calls, criticizing his parents' possessiveness and unreasonable demands, and instructing her husband as to how he should stand up to them. In the new pattern, Suzanne stayed out of her husband's negotiations with his parents, while speaking clearly to the issues that directly concerned her. She let John know, for example, that it was important for her to have time alone with him, and she explained how stressful she found their visits when they spent all their time with family. John did end up telling his parents that he and Suzanne would be staying three of the eight evenings in a hotel together, because they wanted some time alone. Suzanne also took responsibility to ensure her own time away from John's family when she felt she needed it. If John had insisted on staying all eight nights with his family, Suzanne would have decided she could live with it, or she would have made alternative arrangements.

It was a real challenge for John to begin to establish some limits and boundaries with his parents when the "togetherness force" seemed overwhelming. Likewise, Suzanne was challenged to move *toward* her family when the "separateness force" went into full swing. It was this work, however, which ultimately allowed them to stop fighting and find their own comfortable balance between the forces of separateness and togetherness in their lives together.

The Moral of the Story

We may not identify with the specifics of Suzanne's story. Gender roles being what they are, it is far more com-

mon that *he* distances and *she* seeks more togetherness—and
that daughters, not sons, will struggle harder around issues
of caretaking and family responsibility.

Nevertheless, Suzanne's struggle is universal. All of us
come from a "different culture," with family roles and rules
that have evolved over many generations. Whether the issues
are the big ones (How are aging parents cared for? How is
money managed? How are children disciplined?), the medium ones (Is it OK to complain, boast, or shine?), or the
small ones (Do the onions get chopped or sliced?), we are all
deeply affected by family patterns and traditions that may
seem like Truth itself, rather than one perspective among
many.

*In particular, we may fail to appreciate differences in the
patterned ways that individuals move in relationships under stress.*
If our style of managing a stressful event is to share feelings
and seek greater togetherness, we may rail against that other
person whose preferred mode of handling the same stress is
to be more private and self-reliant. If we tend to shift into an
overresponsible, "fix-it" mode when anxiety hits, we may get
all ruffled about that other person who reacts to stress with
underresponsibility or a bit of spaciness. And the more intensely we do *our* thing, the more they do *theirs*. Distancers
distance more when they are pursued. Underfunctioners
underfunction more around overfunctioners. And vice
versa. And the more we get focused on the other person's
behavior rather than our own, the more stuck we become.

The higher the level of anxiety in a relationship and the
longer it continues, the more likely we are to become polarized around differences and to get locked into a rigid and
entrenched position over time. We tend to manage anxiety
by dividing into two camps, quickly losing our ability to see
both sides (or better yet, *more* than two sides) of an issue.

A good illustration of this is the story of one couple who came to therapy on the verge of divorce. Their only child, a six-year-old daughter, had been physically disabled in a car accident two years earlier. During the same year, the father's father was diagnosed with Alzheimer's. Clearly, the level of anxiety in this family had been chronically high, and the child, Deborah, was now having emotional problems at school.

The parents—seeking help for the first time, at the initiation of the school counselor—were hardly able to talk together. "I can't stand being around my wife anymore!" the husband explained. "It's all doom and gloom—always going over how depressed she is about the accident, always talking about Deborah's problems, always acting like someone's died when nobody has died." From the wife's perspective: "My husband can't deal with his feelings, he won't talk about what's happened, he just wants to be away as much as possible. I can't stand being so alone with it."

This couple had become rigidly polarized in dealing with their daughter's disability. Both were out of touch with an important part of their own experience that was being carried by the other in an exaggerated form. The mother was drowning in her grief. The father was distancing from his feelings and insisting that they get on with their lives. In listening to their angry criticisms of each other, one might easily lose sight of the fact that *both* have to grieve and *both* have to get on with their lives—although not in the same ways or on the same timetable.

Reactivity: Toning It Down

Our own *reactivity* to differences is what leads us to exaggerated and stuck positions in relationships—positions that become so rigid and polarized that we lose our ability to relate to *both* the competence and incompetence in the other party —and to *both* the competence and incompetence in the self. Instead we become *overfocused* on the incompetence of the other and *underfocused* on the incompetence of the self. We are unable to see more than one side of an issue, to generate new options, and to observe and change our *own* part in a relationship pattern that is keeping us stuck.

We all get reactive at times, and we know it when it hits. That other person only has to step off the plane, enter the room, come home ten minutes late, or mention a particular subject, and we feel that clutching in the gut, that quick rise of anger, that sudden depressed feeling, or that heavy grip on the heart. Suzanne experienced an intense and automatic emotional response whenever she heard her husband pick up the telephone to call his family in New York. And the couple whose daughter was disabled in a car accident experienced it almost every time they were in the same room together and tried to talk about their child. Our reactivity may take the form of a migraine headache or an attack of diarrhea on the first or last day of every visit home. The more we get stuck in a reactive mode over time, the more our differences become exaggerated and polarized.

Legally Divorced—Emotionally Married

Consider June and Tom, who were like many divorced couples, legally but not emotionally separated. The differences between them were quickly apparent to even the casual observer. June managed anxiety by *overfunctioning*, which is typical for her sibling position as the oldest of four daughters. That is, when stress hit, she moved in quickly in an overresponsible fashion to take charge and fix the situation. The higher the anxiety, the more she functioned harder and harder, and the more she focused on others who did not fulfill their responsibilities or accomplish things. People who were fond of June admired her competence, maturity, and reliability. Those who didn't like her called her bossy, strict, overly assertive, and demanding. This portrait is typical of an older sister of sisters.

Unlike June, Tom *underfunctioned* under stress. He tended to become fuzzy and irresponsible, inviting others to criticize or take over for him. For example, he would tell June that he'd return the kids to her house by 6:00 P.M. Sunday evening, but he would show up at 6:40 instead. Rarely did he make it to the phone to let her know he'd be late, although he knew that lateness pushed June's buttons more than anything else. People who liked Tom admired his warm, laid-back, charming, and relaxed style. Those who weren't his fans thought he should grow up and become more reliable and thoughtful toward others. Tom, in many ways, was a typical youngest child.

June and Tom's respective life-styles also reflected their differences. June was an ambitious and successful real estate agent who was not apologetic about the fact that she enjoyed the finer things in life. Status and material comforts were important to her, and she worked hard to provide the best for herself and her children. Tom, in contrast, worked for low pay with retarded children, and he prided himself on his antimaterialistic values. His company of choice was a group of local artists, all of whom lived modestly.

When I first saw Tom and June in consultation, they were angrily focused on each other, as they had been for much of their marriage. They could sit in the same room together only because of their shared concern about their two children, a son and a daughter, who were both showing signs of emotional difficulties. During our first few sessions together, each blamed the other for "causing" the children's problems. June was convinced that Tom's irresponsibility and immaturity were a terrible influence, especially on the younger child, their son. Tom felt similarly about June's values and life-style ("Can you imagine buying a seventeen-year-old girl a new sports car? What is she trying to prove to that kid!").

The differences between June and Tom had once drawn them together. Tom, who had grown up in an unpredictable family, saw in June the stability and reliability he had yearned for. June, once a quiet, overresponsible child, saw Tom as someone who would teach her to loosen up and have fun. But as it happens, the differences that attracted them to each other became very quickly the focus of angry attention.

Now, eighteen years after marrying and six years after divorcing, their reactive anger *was the glue that kept June and Tom from really separating or divorcing in the emotional sense.* As long as they kept this up, they were as married as ever. Their reactivity to each other kept them close (albeit in a negative way), and neither was ready to let go.

Who was the villain and who the victim? June's friends sided with her, and Tom's friends sided with him. In fact, both Tom and June were competent enough parents and neither of their life-styles was inherently bad for themselves or for their kids. They were just different. Likewise, over-functioning and underfunctioning are normal, patterned ways of managing anxiety. When we get locked into extreme or polarized positions, however, we begin to operate at a cost to both self and other.

So with two kids headed for serious trouble, what was the problem and whose problem was it? The problem was *not* the individual traits, qualities, or values of either parent. Both Tom and June had their strengths and weaknesses.

Rather the problem was their *reactivity* to each other, which was unrelenting and intense.

For example, when Tom brought the kids home an hour late, June might say nothing, but the tension in the room was so thick that her daughter said she could feel it. Five minutes later she would be on the phone with her best friend, talking about how irresponsible and immature Tom was, and how worried she was about his influence on the children. June had all but lost her ability to focus on and relate to Tom's competence as a father.

Tom, of course, did his full share to keep the intensity going. Not only did he know exactly how to push his ex-wife's buttons and keep her involved (like not phoning when he'd be late), but he was also highly reactive to June. For example, when his kids went camping with him and his buddies, wearing the sixty-dollar hiking boots that June had bought for them, Tom all but had a fit. Several times during the camping trip, he took potshots at the "rich kids' boots," which of course was really criticism of the children's mother.

What about the kids? They in turn were reactive to their parents' reactivity. The younger one in particular was becoming increasingly anxious and angry as he struggled with the question of "whose camp" he was in. Unable to navigate a separate relationship with each parent, free from the intensity between them, he was acting up in school and getting into every sort of trouble.

Tom and June quit their work with me after several sessions. Months later, June called to let me know that she had placed her two children in individual psychotherapy and that she hoped this would give them a chance to work on their problems, which she believed her husband had caused. Tom was vehemently against this therapy and refused to drive the kids to their sessions or support it in any way.

According to June, the new therapist joined her in viewing the children as the appropriate focus for treatment and Tom as the irresponsible parent who was not acting in their interests. The negative intensity between Tom and June had escalated to the highest point in their relationship. I do not know whether things are better or worse at the present time.

This is a story about a *child-focused triangle* and later we will be taking a careful look at how such triangles operate. The story also illustrates how different people (including different experts) will *name the problem* in different ways. At this point, however, I am sharing Tom and June's situation to illustrate a few key points.

First, differences per se are rarely "the problem" in relationships; the problem is instead our reactivity to differences. In divorce, for example, kids can do just fine even when the parents have dramatically different values, life-styles, and ways of managing anxiety. Children do poorly, however, when reactivity or expressed emotional intensity is high between the parents, and even more so if they are the focus of it. And of course, the parents stay stuck as well.

Second, reactivity exaggerates and calcifies differences. For example, June's overfocus on her husband's incompetence (and her underfocus on her own issues) only provoked his irresponsible behavior further, and helped polarize their relationship. Similarly, Tom's angry focus on his ex-wife's materialism (and his need to prove himself the "opposite") made it far less likely that the two of them could be in touch with whatever values, beliefs, and desires they did hold in common. Naturally, the kids felt pressured to choose whether they would be "like Dad" or "like Mom" (an impossible loyalty struggle), rather than being able to identify with whatever aspects of both parents felt comfortable to them.

Toning down our reactivity is perhaps the most crucial and difficult step toward removing barriers to intimacy or toward solving any human problem. This is why I sent Suzanne to the library to learn more about ethnicity—so that she could start *thinking* about differences in her marriage rather than just reacting to them. It is also why I challenged her to get better connected with her own family of origin— so that distance and cutoff in this area would not leave her more vulnerable to intense reactions in her marriage or in any other primary relationship. As we have seen with Susan, and Adrienne as well, *change occurs only as we begin thinking about and working on the self—rather than staying focused on and reactive to the other.*

What exactly does it mean to become less reactive and less focused on your ex-husband's irresponsibility, your husband's depression, your boss's criticalness, your brother's distance, your father's drinking, your mother's complaining? By accepting and appreciating differences, are we simply accommodating to a relationship? Does it mean that "anything goes"? Does it mean that we stew inside and say nothing? *Of course not!*

Toning down our reactivity and getting unfocused from the other does *not* mean distance, cutoff, silence, or accommodation. It does *not* mean ignoring things that trouble us, because we are scared of making the situation worse. In fact, toning down our reactivity means putting *more* energy into reconnecting and defining where we stand on important relationship issues, but in a new way that is focused on the self, not on the other. Let's see how this works.

7

Defining a Bottom Line

"I used to get really reactive to my father's drinking," Kristen explained in group therapy, "but I've finally gotten out of that position." Kristen was sharing her story with Alice, another group member who was still trying to "cure" her husband's alcoholism.

"I learned the hard way," Kristen continued, "that I just can't change him. I mean I tried for about ten years. I gave him calm and logical advice. I had screaming fits. I begged and pleaded. I told him that he had a disease that was ruining the whole family. Twice my mom and I signed him up for a treatment program and dragged him down there. Nothing worked. It took me about a decade to come to terms with the fact that I can't stop my dad from drinking and that he's not going to change."

Alice was listening with rapt attention. She knew all too well that her own practice of emptying the liquor bottles down the drain wasn't working, and she was eager for advice. "So how do you handle your father's drinking now?" she asked.

"I just ignore it," Kristen said flatly. "I was home last weekend and I knew right away that Dad had been drinking. I arrived after lunch and he was already slurring his speech and looking terrible. On Sunday he could hardly carry on a conversation and he was pretty much out of it the whole time I was there. When he was down in the basement, my mother told me that he's drinking more and more—and he won't even go to the doctor for a checkup. Dad still denies that he has a serious problem. But I don't get into it with him. I've really come to terms with the fact that I can't help him."

"You mean that you ignore your father's drinking?" asked Alice. "You don't pay attention to it?"

"Yes," explained Kristen. "It took me a long time to learn that there is nothing else I can do. He drinks, and that's his choice. And if you're still trying to make your husband stop drinking, you won't get anywhere, either!"

Kristen's story is a common one that is by no means specific to alcoholism. It raises the broader problem of how we respond in relationships when a person close to us is a chronic underfunctioner, or behaves in ways we cannot easily accept or tolerate. What works for us and what doesn't?

When we are able to recognize and truly accept what does *not* work we are almost halfway along. Kristen shared with the group what she learned that did not work with her dad. What did not work was her being reactive to his drinking and staying anxiously focused on it. What did not work was her giving him advice about his problem or trying to solve it for him. What did not work was her trying to fix or rescue him in any way—or even thinking that this was possible. What did not work was her lying, excusing, or covering up his drinking to any other person. What did not work was criticism, accusation, or blame. As Kristen herself explained, it took her a decade to truly accept that these old behaviors did not work.

And indeed, they do not. Whether the issue is the other person's drinking, depression, irresponsibility, schizophrenia, or whatever—any or all of the aforementioned behaviors only reduce the likelihood that the other person will take responsibility to solve the problem. It may take some of us more than a decade—perhaps a whole lifetime—to truly own up to the fact that these behaviors just don't work. In fact, they operate at the expense of the underfunctioning party and compromise any possibility of closeness based on mutual regard.

Recognizing that the old ways don't work gives us an opportunity to stop, think, gather information, orient to the facts, and generate new options for our own behavior. But to do this in an anxious emotional field is an unusual if not remarkable achievement. When Kristen tried to change the old pattern, what "solution" did she adopt? By her own report, she now ignored her father's behavior entirely—a form of emotional distancing. As we know, distancing from an issue or a person is still a reactive position, driven by anxiety. It simply keeps the intensity underground in one place, leaving us more vulnerable and reactive elsewhere.

Staying silent, acting as if "nothing was happening" when her father was drunk, taking no position on an important issue that bothered her and still made her clutch inside —these are reactive rather than responsible positions in an important relationship.

Kristen now talked *about* her dad with her mom, but she did not talk *to* him, which only further entrenched the long-standing distance between them. Kristen was participating in a common family triangle in which mother and daughter consolidate their closeness through their disappointment and frustration with Dad, rather than each continuing to deal directly with him on their own relationship issues. Father, as well, participates fully in maintaining his outside, underfunctioning position in this triangle.

Kristen's relationship with her father, like Adrienne's relationship with Frank (Chapter 5), reflects two typical patterned ways of managing anxiety. Surely we can recognize these from our own experience: The first is an *overtly* reactive position, where much life energy (anger energy and/or worry energy) is focused on the other, in unsuccessful attempts to change or blame that person; the second is a *covertly* reactive one, where we avoid the experience of intensity by distancing from an individual or a particular issue. When these become ongoing rather than temporary ways of managing anxiety, we are bound to stay stalled.

Where, then, is the middle ground between overfunctioning and overresponsibility on the one hand, and distance and disengagement on the other?

Taking a Position

After long, hard work on Kristen's part, she arrived at a point where she could effectively *define a bottom line* in relationship to her dad and his drinking. What specifically did this entail?

First, Kristen stopped pretending that she was blind to her father's alcoholism, and she took a clear position that she would not stay in his home or talk to him on the phone if he was drinking. She was able to do this in a relatively calm, nonblaming way, *clarifying that she was acting for herself rather than for or against her dad.* Taking this position was difficult for Kristen on a number of counts, down to such details as having to arrange an alternate sleeping plan if she arrived with her kids at her parents' home after a four-hour drive and found her father drunk. With help from group therapy and an Adult Children of Alcoholics group, Kristen was able to stay on track—or more accurately, to get back on track following derailments.

For example, when her dad slurred his words on the phone and called it "a bad cold," Kristen said calmly, "Dad, you say you haven't been drinking, but I'm not able to carry on a conversation with you now. I'm hanging up the phone. Good-bye." When her dad was sober, Kristen worked hard to avoid the old guilt-inducing statements about *him* ("Why do you do this to us!") or about some *other* party ("Do you realize how much you upset Mother last weekend?"). Instead Kristen tried to stick with *"I" statements*—nonblaming statements about the self.

On one weekend visit, for example, Kristen canceled her plans to stay at her parents' home. Instead, she took herself and her children to a nearby motel after dinner because her father was obviously under the influence of alcohol. In a low-keyed way, Kristen made clear to her own kids why she had decided not to stay at her parents' home when her dad had been drinking. Later that week she communicated the following to her father:

"When you've been drinking, Dad, I'm going to do my best to stick to my plan to leave. It's not that I don't care about you. It's that I *do* care about you. I know that I can't do a thing to help you, but it's too painful for me to see that you've been drinking and especially to be reminded that I may not have you around for a very long time."

When her father became defensive, accusing her of exaggerating and making mountains out of molehills, Kristen heard him out and said, "Dad, I don't agree. I obviously see the problem as far more serious than you do—and you certainly know my beliefs about the need for treatment. In any case, I just feel too tense inside to be around you when I even *suspect* you've been drinking. So even if I *do* overreact at times, I'm still going to pick up and go, like I did last Saturday night."

Getting Put to the Test

In a chronically anxious emotional field such as this one, it is an extremely difficult challenge to think rather than react, especially when the "tests" and countermoves start rolling in. Late one night, Kristen's father called her from a phone booth about twenty minutes from her home. He had been in town that day on business and obviously was in no shape to drive home. Kristen immediately phoned her mother, who became hysterical and instructed Kristen to get her father right away, before he killed himself or someone else. But Kristen (who had been in this situation before) had already told her dad that she wasn't going to bail him out anymore when he drank, because it was too hard on her and not an acceptable way to have a relationship with him.

At this point, Kristen became so anxious that she could not think clearly, if at all. She knew that the old pattern of rescuing her dad did not work. At the same time, she wanted to respond appropriately to a situation of imminent danger. Kristen made another call, this time to the leader of her group of Adult Children of Alcoholics, which enabled her to calm down and make a plan. The outcome was that she called the police and explained the situation. She then called her mother to tell her that she had called the police. The police picked up her dad. And Kristen began steeling herself for the volcanic reaction from her folks that would now come her way.

"How Can You Do This to Dad??!!"

And so it goes. Countermoves and "Change back!" reactions are par for the course when we change our part in an old pattern, but knowing this fact may not make the situation any easier to deal with. Both of Kristen's parents acted enraged at her, if not ready to disown her. They attacked her on the phone in such a vitriolic manner that Kristen could barely refrain from hanging up. How dare she humiliate the family this way? Was she aware of the harm she had done to her father's driving record and to his professional reputation? Did she care about the expensive fine that she had imposed on him? What kind of daughter calls the police on her own father?

Kristen felt such a strong rise of anger on the phone that she knew she should wait to respond. She wanted to scream that *she* had not done this to her father, *he* had brought it on himself, and that his taking responsibility for the consequences of his actions was long overdue. But she resisted saying all this, because she knew from experience that it would only fuel the fire.

Instead, Kristen listened for as long as she could tolerate it. Then she told her parents that she needed to get off the phone, but would think about what they had said and then get back to them. "Don't bother!" were her father's last angry words. He was obviously quite sober.

Meeting intensity with more intensity—meeting reactivity with more reactivity—only escalates things further. Instead, Kristen wrote her parents a chatty, informative letter that began by sharing some news about her daughter's recent performance on the soccer field.

Then she addressed the hot issue in a *brief paragraph*, avoiding lengthy explanations and justifications that would only have added to the intensity. Kristen was direct and factual. She did not back down from her bottom line.

First, Kristen apologized for whatever grief, fines, and humiliation that she had caused her dad by calling the police, explaining that certainly it wasn't her intention to hurt him or cause trouble for the family: "I simply didn't see any other alternative," she wrote, "and I still don't. I wasn't going to come get you myself, because I've learned that I just can't do that and still have a relationship with you that feels acceptable to me. And I sure wasn't going to do nothing when I was feeling so scared that you might drive and be in danger. So I did the only thing I could think of, which was to call the police. Frankly, I'd do it again, because I wouldn't know what else to do." When Kristen's older brother got in on the act (*"How could you do such a thing to Dad!"*), she provided him with the same brief explanation.

Mother's Reaction

To Kristen's surprise, the family member who reacted most strongly to her changed behavior was her mother. Yet her mother's reaction was normal and predictable. For one thing, *all* family members (including ourselves) react with anxiety when a family member challenges an old pattern by moving differently. Understandably, Kristen's mother felt especially threatened *because her daughter's new behavior brought her face-to-face with her own position (or lack of position) vis-à-vis her husband's drinking.* It challenged her mother's deeply held belief that she was doing all she could, that nothing else was possible.

Over the long years of her marriage, Kristen's mother had increasingly put more and more energy into focusing on her husband's alcoholism and less and less energy into figuring out how she might live her own life as well as possible. She overfunctioned for her husband (bailing him out and pulling up slack for him) and she underfunctioned for herself (neglecting to clarify her own life goals and failing to set clear limits about what was and was not acceptable to her in regard to her husband's drinking behavior and what she would and would not do). Learning that alcoholism was a disease, she then used this belief to take no position regarding her husband's *management* of his disease. *She had no bottom line,* meaning that she engaged in endless cycles of fighting, complaining, and blaming, but she was unable to say, "These are the things that I cannot and will not tolerate in this relationship." Because Kristen's mother was truly convinced that she could not live *without* her marriage, she could not navigate clearly *within* it.

Kristen's mother did occasionally threaten divorce, but her ultimatums were reactive positions at times of high intensity ("Damn it! If you do this one more time, I'm leaving!"). Often they were expressions of desperation and last-ditch attempts to get her husband to shape up. *In contrast, a bottom-line position evolves from a focus on the self, from a deeply felt awareness (which one cannot fake, pretend, or borrow) of one's own needs and the limits of one's tolerance.* One clarifies a bottom line not primarily to change or control the other person (although the wish may certainly be there), but rather to preserve the dignity, integrity, and well-being of the self. There is no "right" bottom line for all individuals, but if we have *no* bottom line, a relationship (be it with a parent, child, co-worker, friend, lover, or spouse) can only become increasingly chaotic and impaired. This is so, whether we are convinced that the other person's behavior has been caused by illness, poor environment, bad genes, slothfulness, or evil spirits.

For almost four decades, Kristen's mother had participated in a dance with her husband that had high costs for all involved, and she had convinced herself that she had "tried everything." Kristen's new ability to de-intensify her anxious focus on her father's alcoholism, while clarifying a bottom line relative to his drinking behaviors and their relationship, struck at the heart of her mother's core beliefs, assumptions, and behavior. It challenged her mother's very reality of *how things are and how they must be.* It stirred her mother's deepest feelings about her *own* growing up.

Kristen's maternal grandparents had virtually sacrificed their lives for a son who was diagnosed as chronically mentally ill, exhausting themselves to the bone by tolerating all sorts of outrageous and irresponsible behaviors without setting clear limits and boundaries. They, too, saw no options ("We can't put our own son out on the street, can we?") and they blamed him (or his bad genes) for trapping them in an unhappy life. Professional help and community support were unavailable and the advice they did receive ("Kick him out if it's too hard for you") was not useful to them.

Kristen's mother repeated the family pattern—this time with a spouse—and accepted the family "reality" ("One cannot have a clear bottom line with a sick family member"). By replicating this pattern, Kristen's mother was able to deny the repressed rage she felt at the situation in her first family, which had been entirely organized and focused around her sick brother. By *doing the same,* Kristen's mother was proving to herself that nothing different could have been done, that there was no other way. And needless to say, it is a very difficult challenge for any of us to be able to set limits, rules, and boundaries in a solid fashion if our own parents were not able to do this with each other, with us, and with other family members.

The more we know about the broader multigenerational picture, the more we can begin to appreciate the enormity of the change Kristen was making. One does not challenge the legacy of generations without stirring up profound emotionality. It was predictable for Kristen's mother to become anxious about her daughter's new behavior and to express her anxiety by redirecting her anger and blame toward Kristen. It was Kristen's job to manage her mother's reactions without cutting her off or getting pulled back into the old pattern. Dealing with countermoves is what real change is all about.

If only change could take place in one hit-and-run maneuver—but it just doesn't work that way. It's a process that requires us to hang in as best we can. Following Kristen's call to the police, everyone's anxiety was up—and it was understandable that Kristen had difficulty staying in touch with family members who were angrily attacking her or giving her the cold shoulder. If Kristen was serious about real, substantive change, however, she would need to be creative in finding some way to stay in reasonable contact with her father and mother, retreating into distance only temporarily, when necessary.

If Kristen *had* cut off, a new, more functional relationship pattern would not have been established. And if her father's countermove was particularly dramatic (such as injuring himself in a car accident), Kristen's anxiety and guilt about her new position might have been unmanageable if she had failed to find some way to stay responsibly connected. Although the *actual* risk of serious injury or tragedy is far greater with the old pattern, this point is still an important one.

Most important of all, the ability to stay responsibly connected to family members, and to define a solid self in this arena, helps us to bring a more solid self to other intimate relationships. When family relationships have been especially painful and when there are cutoffs in the previous generations, maintaining connectedness is not easy. *But distance or cutoff from family members is always a trade-off.* The plus is that we avoid the strong uncomfortable feelings that contact with certain family members inevitably evokes. The costs are less tangible but no less dear. Family connectedness, even when these relationships are anxious and difficult, is a necessary prerequisite to conducting one's own intimate relationships free from serious symptoms over time and free from excessive anxiety and reactivity. The more we manage intensity by cutting off from members of our own kinship group (extended family included), the more we bring that intensity into other relationships, especially into those with children, if we have them. In some situations it can take years to figure out how to reconnect with a particular family member, but if we can slowly move in this direction rather than in the direction of more cutoff, there are benefits to the self and the generations to come.

Kristen's story had the kind of ending we all like to hear about. Her mother eventually sought help for her "codependency." Her Dad *did* get a handle on his drinking problem, and all the family members began to conduct their relationships more functionally. Not infrequently, this happens. And not infrequently, it doesn't. What is most relevant about this story is *not* that Kristen's changes eventually evoked positive changes on her parents' part. Rather, Kristen defined a responsible position in her family for her self —one that would put *her* on firmer footing for all her relationship ventures and one that would maximize other family members' chances of making use of their own competence.

Don't Just Do Something—Stand There!

The most useful thing you can do in response to Kristen's story is *only to think about it*. People commonly try to make changes they are not ready for or attempt to address a hot issue before they have competently addressed smaller problems. After you have read this book in its entirety, you will be better able to assess what, where, when, and if you wish to change. Surely we do not begin at the most difficult place.

Kristen's story illustrates the most difficult kind of change. Keep in mind, though, that between the "before" and "after" of her story, Kristen had the advantage of participating in both group therapy and in a group of Adult Children of Alcoholics. Clarifying a new position with her dad was not something she just decided to jump into one day. For all of us, such changes require careful preparation, planning, and practice, and in some cases, professional help.

What you can do, though, is to use Kristen's story as a springboard to thinking about your own pattern of responding to an underfunctioning person or to a significant other whose behavior is not acceptable to you. We will continue to learn more about the process of defining a self in relationships, and the implications of having or not having a bottom line. For now, keep in mind that patience is a priority; we can't learn to swim by jumping off the high dive.

Kristen's story does give us much to think about *that is not specific to having an alcoholic family member.* The changes Kristen made illustrate her struggle to *define a self* within the intense emotional field of family relationships. This struggle is relevant, indeed central, to all of our lives. And since we cannot hold the clock still, we are always navigating relationships in the direction of greater or lesser degrees of self.

We all do better in life when we can stay reasonably connected to important others; when we can listen to them without trying to change, convince, or fix; and when we can make calm statements about how we see things, based on thinking, rather than reacting. We all do better when we can process an important issue (in Kristen's case, her dad's drinking) and take a clear position rather than relying on silence or blame. We all do better when we have a clear bottom line ("I am not able or willing to live with these behaviors") rather than communicating through our own behavior that "anything goes." We all do better when we can deal directly with our most difficult family members rather than talking about them with other relatives. And finally, we all do better when we can de-intensify our anxious focus on the other's problem and put our primary energy into clarifying our own beliefs, convictions, values, and priorities, while formulating plans and life goals that are congruent with these.

Kristen's story illustrates some key aspects of defining a self. But there is more. Defining a whole and authentic self also means sharing *both* our overfunctioning and underfunctioning sides with significant others rather than participating in polarized relationships where we stay focused on the other person's problems but do not share our own. Every person, *without exception,* has strengths and competencies as well as weaknesses and vulnerabilities, but most of us have difficulty identifying and expressing both sides. This is especially the case when an overfunctioning-underfunctioning polarity gets set in motion and each person's behavior only provokes and maintains the behavior of the other.

It was as difficult for Kristen to consider sharing her underfunctioning side with her father ("Dad, I'm having a problem and I'd like your thoughts about it") as it was for her dad to exercise his competence to stop drinking. An overfunctioning style is very difficult to modify and the costs of overfunctioning are often hidden. For our selves, however, and for those close to us, it is a challenge worth thinking about.

8

Understanding Overfunctioning

Everyone knows that chronic *under*functioners need to change. If we underfunction—as Kristen's father did—we receive the diagnostic labels, get sent to therapy, and get placed in treatment centers or psychiatric hospitals. Our families may identify us as "the sick one," "the spoiled one," "the irresponsible one," "the troublemaker," "the black sheep." People may distance from us or become overfocused on us, often in unhelpful ways. We ourselves may be convinced that we are an emotional basket case, while others in our family seem to have no loose ends.

In contrast, if we *over*function, we may truly believe that God is on our side. Surely, we have done everything possible to be helpful and our greatest source of distress is the other person—who is unable or unwilling to shape up. Unfortunately, those around us may reinforce this attitude, this way of seeing only part of the picture. Or they may do the opposite and blame us for "causing" the problem through our own behavior—a similarly narrow and distorted view.

All of us have relationships and circumstances in which we overfunction, and this is not necessarily problematic, particularly if we can observe it and make a shift. For example, our daughter calls in tears because she was put on probation at work. Instead of asking her questions—or perhaps sharing something from our own experience—we try to lift her spirits or tell her three things to do. Later that day we reflect on the conversation and recognize that our advice was unsolicited and that we really weren't listening very well. So we call her back the next day to simply see how she's doing. We ask a few questions about the job situation and tell her we're sorry she's having such a hard time.

When we get *stuck* in an overfunctioning position, however, we may find change exceedingly difficult. This rigidity exists because overfunctioning is not just a bad habit, a misguided attitude, an overzealous wish to be helpful, or a behavior pattern caused by living with a chronically underfunctioning individual, such as an alcoholic spouse; overfunctioning, like underfunctioning, is a patterned way of managing anxiety that grows out of our experience in our first family and has deep roots in prior generations. This reactive response operates almost instinctually, without conscious awareness or intent. And it can keep us—and our relationships—incredibly stuck.

Those who come by overfunctioning most naturally are often (although by no means always) firstborns or only children. The tendency will be exaggerated if a firstborn has same-sex siblings (the older sister of a sister, the older brother of brothers). And it will be particularly intense if one parent was physically or emotionally unable to competently do his or her job and we stepped in as an overresponsible child—a fixer, a mediator, or the like. Because overfunctioners "look good" (like my sister "sailing through" at the time of my mother's cancer diagnosis), their needs and problems are often overlooked, even by themselves. That is until they get good and sick—or find some other way to collapse. It may take nothing less than a serious emotional or physical illness for a chronic overfunctioner to slow down and force attention to her own needs. And when overfunctioners *do* collapse under the strain of overfunctioning, they can do it in a big way.

Defining Our Terms

As we have seen, *overfunctioning* can be defined as *an individual's characteristic style of managing anxiety and navigating relationships under stress.* If you are a good overfunctioner, you will identify the following characteristics in yourself.

OVERFUNCTIONERS

- know what's best not only for themselves but for others as well.
- move in quickly to advise, fix, rescue, and take over when stress hits.
- have difficulty staying out of and allowing others to struggle with their own problems.
- avoid worrying about their own personal goals and problems by focusing on others.
- have difficulty sharing their own vulnerable, underfunctioning side, especially with those people who they believe have problems.
- may be labeled as people who are "always reliable" or "always together."

Overfunctioning, however, is not simply a description of an individual's defensive style. More to the point, overfunctioning (along with underfunctioning) refers to *a reciprocal (or circular) relationship pattern*. Given sufficient anxiety, the pattern will become polarized and "stuck," as illustrated by the examples of my sister and me. Viewed from this perspective, overfunctioning (like underfunctioning) is an attribute of a *relationship system* that cannot be understood apart from the whole. Let's take a closer look at this way of thinking.

De-Selfing and Pseudo-Self

When Dr. Murray Bowen, founder of Bowen family systems theory, first described the reciprocal pattern of overfunctioning and underfunctioning, he was referring to a common marital process in which one partner gives up self (de-selfing) and the other gains in pseudo-self. The person who sacrifices self is the *underfunctioner*. The person who is bolstered in self is the *overfunctioner*. Just how does this exchange work?

When couples pair up and stay paired up, they are usually at the same level of "self" or independence. That is, the amount of "true self" or "solid self" that they have carved out in their first family—and now bring to their relationship—is about the same. Or, we might say that they are at the same level of emotional maturity. For example, when Jo-Anne (our anonymous letter writer who canceled her subscription to *Ms.* magazine) first married Hank (as we will now call him) their "levels of self" might be depicted by a horizontal line (see figure A on page 106).

If we look at this couple several years down the road, however, their levels of self may *look* more like figure B (see page 106).

Over time, Jo-Anne has assumed the adaptive and un-

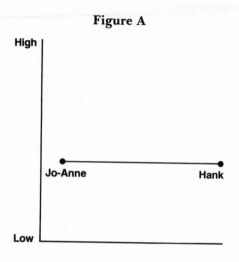

Figure A

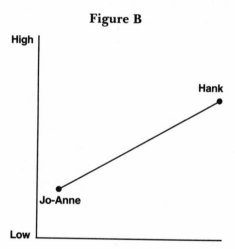

Figure B

derfunctioning role, knuckling under to marital pressures and going along with someone else's program. She may be depressed and symptomatic, without personal and life goals. Hank, in contrast, may have no psychiatric or physical symptoms and may be up for a promotion at work. To all the world, he *appears* to have "more self" than his spouse and to be functioning well. Over time, the polarity may become firmly entrenched. Hank's reactivity to his wife's underfunctioning may take the form of angry distance and/or over-focus—but in either case, he will begin to share less of his *own* problems and vulnerability with her (if he ever did to begin with) and she will share less of her strength and competence with him.

The difference in their levels of functioning, however, is more apparent than real. In systems language, Hank has gained in pseudo-self in proportion to his wife's de-selfed position. She has "given up" self and he has "borrowed self." It's just like a seesaw. If, by some stroke of magic or plain hard work, Jo-Anne were to change in the direction of greater selfhood, we would predictably see this:

Figure C

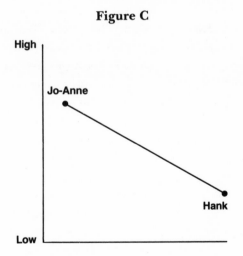

As Jo-Anne began to look better, Hank might get depressed and begin to look worse. Psychotherapists see this

happen routinely, and predictably. We have observed it at
the societal level as well, as when men first complained of
feeling impotent or castrated in response to changes in
women brought about by feminism. It is not simply that the
strengthening of women is *confused* with the weakening of
men. More to the point, the pseudo-self of men is actually
challenged as woman stop giving up self.

If Jo-Anne were able to maintain a genuinely higher
level of "solid self" (as opposed to overfunctioning at
Hank's expense), the seesaw swing depicted in figure C
would not stay static. Hank might ultimately meet the challenge of moving to a higher level of self in response to the
real changes that his wife has made. Or several years down
the road Hank and Jo-Anne may no longer be together.

Why Change?

From where, then, does the overfunctioner find the will
to change? As Kristen's story illustrates, change can be a
profoundly difficult and anxiety-arousing business. As frequently as not, the motivation is just not there or it runs out
after the initial push. And understandably so. Where will we
get the courage, to say nothing of the motivation, to begin to
modify our overfunctioning ways? Why change if we are
sitting at the top of the emotional seesaw, if we can avoid
the full impact of our own unfinished business by focusing
on the other, if we can derive that secret feeling of self-
righteousness from diagnosing others and being "right," or
if we are the "insider" that the family talks *to* ("Let me tell
you what your brother did now!") rather than *about*?

It's a real dilemma. The will *not* to change is often particularly powerful in chronic overfunctioners. First, we tend *not*
to see that we have a problem: We have only tried to be
helpful to that other person, and if we have distanced or cut

off, it is only after being convinced that we have tried all possibilities. Like Kristen and her mother, we cannot see how we are contributing to a painfully stuck relationship pattern because we cannot imagine (and may not really want to imagine) another way of relating. We may even be convinced that the other party cannot survive without our help ("My sister wouldn't eat if I didn't buy her groceries").

Second, we do not know *how* to modify our overfunctioning position. We may have no clear instructions, no well-marked road map, and no trained coach to guide us over the rough spots. In all probability, we may lack a realistic assessment of just how tough the going can get—if we really get going.

Finally, it is *emotionally painful* to modify a chronic overfunctioning pattern. As we will see, it may evoke strong feelings of depression, anxiety, and anger as our own vulnerabilities and needs come rushing to the surface—and who needs that! It's understandably hard to tolerate short-term pain, even for the promise of a more whole and grounded self later on.

Yet some of us do find the will to change, as Kristen's story illustrates. Such change requires us to move against our wish to fix things and our even stronger wish for distance once we find we can't fix things. But perhaps the most difficult aspect of modifying an overfunctioning pattern is to *share our vulnerability* with the underfunctioning person and to *relate to that person's competence*. Let's return to the last part of Kristen's story to see how this can be done—and to appreciate the strong emotionality it evokes.

Back to Kristen

In a later, second incident, Kristen again called the police to collect her father. In response, Kristen's father called her "terribly selfish"—at which point she lost control. In her next group-therapy session, Kristen described the experience: "At that moment, I exploded. *He* was calling *me* selfish! *He* was telling me how *I* hurt the family! I just let the bastard have it. I just couldn't take it anymore, and I didn't care if I was blowing it."

"Blowing it" is a normal part of the difficult process of change. We do not alter our part in a stuck relationship pattern without returning again and again to our old ways. The group empathized with Kristen's feelings and her surge of reactivity. Some thought it was good for her to have let her anger out full force. Most importantly, Kristen was able to get back on course again.

About a month later (and almost a year from her first call to the police), Kristen performed a bold and courageous act. She wrote her father a letter that included the following message.

> Dad, I've been giving some thought to your opinion that I've become selfish, and I've come to the conclusion that you have a point there. I *am* becoming more selfish. To be honest, I'm even *working* on becoming more selfish. I think that I've spent much of my life looking over my shoulder worrying about your drinking, or Mom's problems, and I've put very little energy into getting clear about who I am and where I'm going in my life. Focusing so much on *your* problems may have given me a place to hide, because I didn't have to look too hard at myself and my own problems. Now that I'm thinking about *me*, I realize I've been unhappy with my job situation for a long time and not doing anything about it. At the same time, I'm feeling hopeful because at least I'm starting to think about it.

In a later conversation with her dad, Kristen described a specific problem affecting her at work and also shared her ongoing indecision about career directions. She asked him if he had any thoughts or reactions to her dilemma and also expressed interest in learning whether he had ever struggled with similar issues. How had *he* decided on his particular line of work? Had he ever thought about a career change? What work issues did others in his family struggle with? Kristen let her father know that whatever he could share of his own considerable experience around work issues might help her to struggle more productively with her own decisions. Later that week she talked with her mother about work and career struggles on her mother's side of the family.

Soon thereafter, Kristen became profoundly depressed. Although she said her depression hit her "out of the blue," it was anything but surprising. By sharing her *own* underfunctioning side with her father, Kristen was challenging the roles and rules that constituted her family's "reality." She was changing the rules governing their dance by relating to *his* competence, by considering his perspective of value, by being more of a *self* in their relationship, and by no longer pretending that she had it all together. For example, one of the family's "realities" was that her father, as a "sick" alcoholic, should not be burdened by other family members' problems and surely could have no valuable advice to offer. Another unspoken rule was that fathers and daughters should not have real relationships.

By inviting her father to act like a father, Kristen also unleashed a torrent of buried emotions and unmet dependency needs within herself, needs and longings that she had kept safely blocked from awareness by chronically overfunctioning and overfocusing on the problems of others. Her father's positive response to her self-disclosure paradoxically unleashed her buried rage and disappointment about what she had *not* been able to get from him and her family throughout her lifetime. Her first, gut response was that whatever he could give her now was not enough—and too late.

Kristen could not understand why her new behavior, and her dad's positive response to it, left her feeling more miserable than ever. Her reaction, however, was predictable and par for the course. And it is because change is often *this* difficult that many of us choose to continue with our old ways.

On the other hand, the payoffs are high if we can do this work and stay on course (or more accurately, get back on course) over time. Sharing vulnerability and relating to the other person's competence are essential to restoring balance in a relationship with an underfunctioning individual. If we cannot do this, it is far less likely that the other person will put energy into their own recovery and they will have to work twice as hard to even be in touch with their own competence.

Even more to the point, this work allows us to move toward a more balanced and authentic self. It is our best insurance policy against continuing polarized relationships with new people in our lives and passing the pattern down the generations.

Finally, if we are able to modify a chronic overfunctioning pattern, we will begin to be in touch with the real costs to self of the old way. It is frustrating, exhausting, angering, and draining (both financially and emotionally) to overfunction—to be rescuing, bailing out, pulling up slack, or paying more attention to the problems of others than to one's own. And distancing from that other family member who just isn't doing well doesn't really leave us feeling very solid, responsible, or grounded in the long run, despite our attempts to convince ourselves otherwise.

So far, we have been looking at a *chronic* overfunctioning-underfunctioning pattern. By chronic, I mean that the pattern is fixed and long-standing, with roots that may go back for generations. Resistance to change is sky-high, both from within and without, and professional guidance is often necessary to help us lower reactivity, observe our part in the dance, and stay on course over time. Often the strong feelings stirred by moving differently are so uncomfortable we will tell ourselves we don't want to change, it's not worth it, or it's not possible.

Let's turn now to the story of Anita, who provides a typical example of *mild* overfunctioning that swung into full force at a particularly stressful time in the family life cycle. Anita was able to make changes relatively easily because the "stuckness" that brought her to therapy was only of several months' duration. When a relationship gets stuck in response to an acute reaction to recent stress, change is more manageable.

"I'm Terribly Concerned About Mother!"

Anita was a twenty-nine-year-old administrative nurse who came to see me several months after her seventy-eight-year-old grandmother had a serious fall. Anita was obviously tense and under considerable strain when she entered my office.

When we first talked on the phone, Anita said she was seeking help because of headaches and anxiety spells. But during our first session, she focused almost exclusively on her mother, Helen, who was deeply absorbed in caring for *her* mother, Anita's ailing grandmother.

Anita shared that she had initially felt sympathetic toward her mother's plight, but over time her sympathy had turned to frustration and then to outright anger. "My mother cares for Grandma at the expense of everything else in her life," Anita explained. "She's wearing herself to the bone, she's neglecting Dad, and most important, she's neglecting herself."

When we complain that our mothers (or whoever) won't listen to reason, it usually means that they won't see things our way or do what we want them to do. As with Suzanne and John (Chapter 6), one key issue here was reactivity to differences. Anita was clearly having a hard time accepting the fact that her mother's way of managing a difficult situation differed from her own. Our reactivity to differences will always be higher at particularly stressful points in the life cycle (for example, at a wedding or funeral) because anxiety is the driving force behind reactivity.

For most of Anita's adulthood, she and her mother had shared a close relationship and could talk together openly and comfortably. Their relationship was not too polarized, in that each could share problems and relate to the competence of the other in solving her own difficulties. But when Anita's grandmother's health began deteriorating after her fall, Anita became focused on how her mother was handling this difficult situation. It was during this particularly stressful point that Anita's tendency to overfunction went into full swing and another mother-daughter relationship became stuck.

The Way It Was

In the months after her grandmother's fall, the interaction between Anita and her mother had become increasingly strained. Helen would complain to Anita about her continual exhaustion and about her unrelieved responsibility for her mother. Anita would then suggest ways that Helen could lessen her load; for example, by asking other family members to pitch in or by hiring a nurse to stay with Grandma several hours a day. Helen, in response, would either ignore this advice or tell Anita why her advice would not work. Anita would continue to argue her point, while Helen would continue not to listen.

What did Anita do then? Sometimes she repeated the advice, although her mother was not making use of it. After a while, Anita would distance from her mother ("I just don't want to hear her complaining if she doesn't want to do anything about it"), or she would interpret and diagnose Helen's behavior ("Mother, I think you secretly enjoy being a martyr and doing this super-responsible trip. You keep asking me for advice only to reject it, and that makes me feel angry and helpless"). When they managed to get off the subject of Grandma, their conversation tended to be superficial.

Although Helen was overextending herself for her mother, she was actually underfunctioning in terms of problem solving around the caretaking issue. And the more Anita took on Helen's problem as her own or focused intensely on the issue, the more Helen continued to underfunction for her self. Of course, Helen's behavior invited Anita's overfunctioning, just as Anita's overfunctioning invited her mother's underfunctioning. That's how a reciprocal or circular dance works.

"How much of your worry energy—or emotional energy—is directed toward your mother at this time?" I asked Anita the third time we met. I asked her to be as specific as possible; I wanted a percentage figure.

"About seventy-five percent," she answered quickly. My estimate would have been even higher.

"If that problem were to be magically resolved, if there were absolutely no cause for concern about your mother, where would that seventy-five percent worry energy be going? What else would you be paying attention to?"

"I don't know," Anita said simply. "I've never thought about it."

And indeed, she hadn't.

How Overfunctioning Helps

One of the nice things about any kind of *other-focus* is that we will not experience the full impact of our own issues. Obviously, lots of emotions were stirred up inside Anita in response to her grandmother's downhill slide and the specter of her impending death. How did Anita want to relate to Grandma at this time? How much contact did she want to initiate? What, if any, unfinished business did Anita have with Grandma that she might want to address before it was too late? If Grandma died tomorrow, would Anita feel at peace with this relationship, or would she wish that she had said or asked one thing or another? These are just a few of the questions Anita was able to *not* think about—or not think *too hard* about—because she was thinking about Helen, worrying about Helen, and talking about Helen to her therapist, family, and friends.

Another piece of psychological business that was stirred up for Anita at this time involved the question of a daughter's responsibility to an aging dependent parent. Helen's total and selfless devotion to Grandma made Anita anxious, because she experienced her mother's behavior as an expectation that *Anita would one day do the same*. The notion that Anita would one day devote *her* life to her aging mother or father scared and angered her, although her parents had never voiced any such expectations. Nor had Anita consciously articulated her concerns—even to herself. Instead, Anita made an automatic, reflexive move away from her own anxiety to a worried and critical focus on her mother. That's how people work. And this is how we begin to change it.

New Steps

The first thing Anita was able to do differently was to stop giving advice. Learning how *not* to be helpful is an especially difficult challenge for those of us who move in quickly to fix the problems of other family members or to rescue those in distress. Of course, there is nothing wrong with Anita giving advice to Helen *if* Helen finds it useful and *if* Anita recognizes that her advice may not fit her mother ("Well, this is what I would do in your shoes, but that may not be right for you. What are your thoughts?").

In the old pattern, Anita was giving advice from an overfunctioning or overresponsible position. She was truly convinced she had the answers to her mother's problem, and she became angry when her mother ignored her advice. For this reason Anita would do well to stop giving advice, at least until she can shift to a more respectful position regarding her mother's need to find her own solutions.

When we overfunction for family members, we can be sure they will underfunction for themselves and act less competently to solve their own problems. Furthermore, Anita already knows that her mother resists her advice. Doing more of the same can only keep Anita more stuck.

When Anita was ready to break the old pattern, she stopped trying to change her mother and began to change her own responses. When Helen called and complained about feeling drained by Grandma's illness, Anita asked questions and listened empathetically. She did not advise her mother in any way. Anita's attitude conveyed respect for the fact that her mother was the best expert on herself and that she was struggling with a truly wrenching dilemma.

It Doesn't Mean Silence!

What do overfunctioners do when they get angry, frustrated, and exhausted? As we have seen, they typically move into a position of reactive distance. I speak here not just of physical distance ("I just won't call or write him anymore") but also of emotional distance around the issue of concern. Kristen, for example, initially confused distance with substantive change on her part when she went from trying to fix her father's drinking behavior to acting as if it were not happening.

Clarifying our position around an important issue is always a key part of defining the self. Anita learned to do this *by saying something about her own self rather than trying to be the expert on her mother.* After a telephone conversation in which Helen again presented herself as exhausted and stressed-out, Anita responded: "You know, Mother, your ability to take care of Grandma truly amazes me. If it were me, I simply couldn't do it. I would have to find some way to get help and get time for myself, no matter what it took."

When her mother responded by giving a dozen reasons why help was not possible, Anita did not argue the point. She just said again, "You know, Mother, I just couldn't do it. I'm not saying I have the answers for you. I'm just saying that I could not be doing so much for anyone, no matter how much I loved them. I don't think I'd even be physically capable of it. But I recognize that you and I are different."

Anita stayed on track, although she often had to bite her tongue to avoid going back to the old pattern of advice-giving and arguing. Over lunch several weeks later, Helen told Anita that caring for Grandma was taking a toll on her own health. At this point, Anita turned to her mother and said warmly, "Mom, I've always admired how good you are at taking care of everyone. Your ability to keep giving to others never ceases to amaze me. You've taken care of three children. And you've taken care of Dad. And when Uncle Harry was in trouble, you were the first to be there to take care of him. And now you're taking care of Grandma.

"But there's only one problem. Who is taking care of you, Mom? This is what I worry about sometimes. Who's taking care of Helen?"

Helen became teary, and Anita suddenly realized that she had never seen her mother cry. Helen told Anita that no one really took much care of her and that furthermore she probably wouldn't allow it. She talked some about her own childhood and how her father's early death had left her feeling that it wasn't safe to depend on anyone. When they parted that afternoon, Anita knew her mother better.

What allowed this conversation to happen was Anita's ability to share her genuine concern for her mother without going back to her overfunctioning pattern (which was similar to her mother's pattern) of advising, rescuing, or fixing. Anita was sharing from the self, without implying what Helen should think, feel, or do, and without telling her specifically how she should solve her problem. Not long thereafter, her mother did begin to use her competence to make a change in her situation. The solution wasn't one Anita would have chosen, but it offered Helen some relief.

The change on Anita's part was not just a strategic shift into "I" language. It came from a deeper place, from a growing recognition that we cannot know for sure what is best for another person—what they can and cannot tolerate, what they need to do, when, and why. Surely it is difficult enough to know this for one's own self.

The Hardest Part

In Anita's case, the challenge of sharing her own anxieties and issues with her hitherto focused-on mother was a manageable challenge, because she and Helen had had an open and flexible relationship before the crisis created by her grandma's ill health. And so, sitting together on a park bench one fall afternoon, Anita began to tell Helen what had been stirred up inside her in response to the recent events. Mother and daughter were able to talk about their reactions to Grandma's deteriorating health, and cried some together. This sharing of emotions contrasts with emotional reactivity, which is an anxiety-driven response. Anita also asked her mother *directly* if she, Helen, would expect the same kind of caretaking from her children in her old age that Helen was now giving to Grandma. Anita's anxiety was much alleviated as she and her mother talked openly about the subject; Anita no longer had to float around in her own fantasies and fears.

Easy conversations? No. But Anita had an easier job than many of us would, because the stuck relationship pattern that brought her into therapy was an acute reaction to the anxious emotional field created by Grandma's ill health. Prior to this crisis, she and her mother had had a mature and flexible relationship where each preserved a high degree of separate self. This meant that they could listen to the other's problems—*and stay in their own skin*—without rushing in to fix things and without getting too nervous about differences. They could give advice or feedback, when appropriate, but each could also relate to the competence of the other to find solutions to her own problems. They could state their own opinion on any issue, while leaving room for the view of the other. This makes the process of change about as easy as it gets. Which actually, from Anita's perspective, was not particularly easy at all.

At times of high stress, all of us can get stuck in an other-focused position. The process may be a temporary and circumscribed reaction, as in Anita's case, or it may evolve into an extreme, overfunctioning-underfunctioning polarity, as in Kristen's family. Or we may be somewhere along this continuum of acute to chronic, somewhere between "mild stuckness" and a carved-in-stone polarity.

In my first family, my sister, Susan, and I participated in an overfunctioning-underfunctioning polarity that was linked to an issue of survival. No wonder that today, some thirty years later, it doesn't take too much anxiety to get us back into doing our old thing. We've both come a long way in working on our part of the pattern, but I presume it will always be a challenge. Had the level of family anxiety been even higher and lasted longer, and had our family possessed fewer emotional resources to manage this anxiety, the challenge for us today would be greater still.

Of course, I have a few conspicuous areas of overfunctioning, just as Susan has significant pockets of underfunctioning. Although every person has a predominant operating style, we will manage anxiety in different ways according to context and circumstance, according to the particular relationship and the specific issue at hand. For example, a woman may be an overfunctioner at work and an underfunctioner in her marriage. Or she may be a chronic distancer with her father and a chronic pursuer with men in her love life. Far from being a "contradiction," my sister's experience with David (Chapter 4) illustrates that a woman's distance from her father (or more specifically, the unaddressed issues and emotionality that are managed by distance) may be what raises anxiety (managed by pursuit) in other intimate relationships.

Anxiety continues to be a key concept in understanding how stuck our relationships will get, how resistant we (and others) will be to change, and how much change can actually be tolerated. We have seen how anxiety locks us into polarized positions in relationships, blocking productive communication and problem solving, and making intimacy impossible to achieve. Anxiety hits us from all directions, moving vertically down the generations and horizontally as we pass through life-cycle events and just plain hard times. As our next example will illustrate, a particular *subject* may itself carry so much anxiety that it is difficult to discuss in an open and respectful way. If a topic feels too hot to handle, we may opt for silence at the expense of authentic connectedness— or we may feel we have to make a choice between having a relationship and being a self.

9

Very Hot Issues:
A Process View of Change

What's a daughter to do about a mother?
When she's the apple of her mother's eye?
    Does she make her mother squirm
    By exposing the worm?
Or does she help her mother deny?

                  "The Daughter's Song"

    Where did I go wrong?
    Am I the one to blame?
    What was it that I did to her
    To bring about this shame?
    How did it happen?
    How could it possibly be?
    That she . . . she . . . she's
    So different
    From me?

               "The Mother's Song"
          Lyrics by Jo-Ann Krestan

Three weeks before her older sister's wedding, Kimberly flew from Kansas City to Dallas and told her parents that she was a lesbian. Mary, her lover of three years, was with her during this self-disclosure. Kimberly's father responded as if he had been struck across the face. He said nothing and left the room. Kimberly's mother wept and then fired accusing questions: "Why are you telling us this?" "How can you sit here and tell me that you are a homosexual?" "Are you getting help for yourself?"

Kimberly's attempts to defend herself fell on deaf ears. After about ten minutes or more of the same, she told her mother that she and Mary were not prepared to listen to insults and that they would stay overnight with a friend. Kimberly left the friend's telephone number on the kitchen table, with a note telling her parents to call if and when they were ready to discuss the subject in a civil fashion. Kimberly heard nothing. She returned to Kansas City and decided she would not recognize her parents' existence if they would not recognize her partner and respect her life choice. She also decided not to attend her sister's wedding, "partly for financial reasons," as she put it. She had already spent enough money on her recent visit home.

About six weeks later, Kimberly's position softened. She decided to give her parents "one more chance." She gathered together some literature on gay and lesbian issues and sent it off to Dallas, with a letter inviting reconciliation. She expressed a wish that her parents would read the material so they could confront their homophobic attitudes and adopt a more informed view.

Kimberly's parents opened the package and resealed and returned it without a word. They did, however, send her a birthday card the following month, signed, "Love, Mom and Dad," but without their usual note and gift. It was at this

point that Kimberly declared herself an orphan, with no
further use for her parents.

For several years prior to "D-Day," as Kimberly later
called it, she had been wanting to share her lesbian identity
with her parents, especially her mother. Although a previous
therapist had encouraged her *not* to tell ("Your parents
don't tell you about their sex life. Why do you feel this
compulsion to tell them about yours?"), Kimberly nonetheless found herself moving in the direction of coming out. She
was aware that keeping such a big secret from her family
ensured that her relationships with both parents could only
remain distant and superficial, colored by silence and lies.
Her invisibility as a part of a couple also affected her relationship with Mary as well.

Kimberly's secret from her family was hardly a circumscribed one involving only "sexual preference," meaning
with whom she was sleeping or to whom she was attracted.
Her lesbian identity also included her primary emotional
commitments, her choice of a woman-centered life-style, and
the everyday details of living, both large and small: from
whom she vacationed with and how she spent her free time,
to her recent role as an active organizer in the lesbian community. The long-term effects of staying closeted not only
precluded the possibility of authentic emotional contact with
family members but slowly eroded Kimberly's sense of dignity and self-regard, as well. It also diminished her energies
and joy (as holding secrets always does) in small, impercepti-
ble, but cumulative ways and negatively affected her relationship with Mary.

Kimberly's decision to come out was an act of courage.
Choosing not to come out, however, does not signify an
absence of the same. As I said earlier, no one can predict the

consequences of change—not for ourselves and surely not for others. We do not know how much change is tolerable for an individual at a particular time, nor how much anxiety she or he can sit with. We cannot really know another person's story. For several years Kimberly had *resisted* pressures from her friends to come out to her family. *Her resistance was also an act of courage,* because Kimberly could recognize that she was not emotionally ready or prepared to make this announcement.

Coming Out: A Woman's Issue

Let's look more carefully at Kimberly's situation, because *coming out is an issue for all women.* We all have emotionally charged issues in our family that are difficult to address. We all may find ourselves confronting a choice between authenticity and harmony in a particular relationship. We all have to deal with powerful countermoves and "Change back!" reactions—both from within and without—if we define the "I" apart from the roles and rules of family and culture. And we all, by virtue of being female, have learned to please and protect relationships by silencing, sacrificing, and betraying the self.

Kimberly's experience will allow us to consolidate some of the lessons we have already learned about defining the "I." Her story teaches us what we can prepare for when we bring up *any emotionally loaded issue* and try to process it with our significant others. It reminds us of the *dilemma of differences* which always threaten as they inform—and which implicitly question the assumptions of the similar. We can count on the subject of lesbianism to be an especially loaded difference for families in our homophobic society.

Keep in mind that emotionally loaded issues come in every shape and form. Some issues, such as incest, are obviously intense. Other issues may not *seem* that hot from an outsider's perspective ("Mom, I've decided to leave the church") but may feel totally untouchable to a particular individual in a particular family. For Adrienne, the facts and feelings surrounding the decision to institutionalize Greg made it an emotionally explosive issue. For Jo-Anne, our anonymous letter writer in Chapter 2, a statement to her husband that she planned to continue her subscription to *Ms.* magazine might be akin to "coming out" and feel no less dangerous. Sometimes a straightforward, factual question ("Dad, how did Uncle Bill actually die?") may take years to lead up to.

Why would we even bother to *think* about tackling a hot issue no one wants to talk about? Why would we *share something* or *ask something* that makes us feel like we are dropping an emotional bomb on our family? Often, we won't. Sometimes, however, our failure to share something —or ask something—greatly impairs our experience of self, our sense of esteem and worth, and our ability to be intimate with significant others. Once again, intensity from a key family relationship does not go away when we manage it through distance and cutoff. It only goes underground.

How do we open up a difficult subject in a way that is ultimately healing, laying the groundwork for greater closeness? How do we avoid a confrontation that only evokes more reactivity and cutoff? These are the questions that Kimberly did *not* think about before she flew home to make her announcements.

"D-Day" Revisited

Kimberly came for therapy nine months after D-Day. The birthday card from her parents was their last communication and Kimberly was still furious at their response. She sought my help because she had heard I was an "anger expert"—and she was angry. At the same time, she was not motivated to reconnect with her family. She just wanted to "work through her anger," whatever that meant—preferably without ever having to *do* anything differently with the people involved.

Kimberly told me that she had disclosed her lesbianism to her parents in hopes of having "real relationships" with them, rather than distant and dishonest ones. But instead of a shifting toward greater intimacy, their relationships had moved from distance to more distance, and now into a period of cold war. What process had occurred—or failed to occur?

It *Is* a Process!

Although Kimberly knew better intellectually, she thought of coming out as something she would go home and "do" ("Well, I've done it!") *rather than as the first small step in a long-term process.* She confused her parents' *initial* response with what might come later from her efforts. Kimberly did not have a process view of change. In fact, she did not even have an objective view of her *own* process. There were many years between Kimberly's *first* acknowledgment of her own different and "bad" feelings and her ultimate positive acceptance of her emotional and sexual orientation to women.

As we have seen, the predictable response to substantive change is increased anxiety followed by countermoves ("Change back, or else . . ."). If we are serious about the work, we need to *anticipate* countermoves and *plan to manage our own reactivity in the face of them.* Countermoves ("You don't mean that!" "How can you be so selfish!") do not mean that our efforts toward change are misguided or have failed. It simply means that the process of change is proceeding along normal lines. It is our job to hold our ground in the face of countermoves, without becoming defensive, without trying to convince others to think or feel differently, and without cutting off.

Counting on Countermoves

Margie, a twenty-six-year-old woman I saw in therapy, said she felt like she was "coming out" when she began to share some of her troubles with her mother. Margie's label in her first family was "Little Miss Sunshine." For as far back as she could remember, she was the "Always-Happy-Child" who would give her mother nothing to worry about, unlike her father who was addicted to gambling and repeatedly involved in unwise business ventures. *It was clear that her mother was highly reactive to the slightest sign of distress in her daughter and was unable to relate to Margie's competence to manage the sadness and depression that life's circumstances inevitably evoke.*

Margie's earliest memory was of returning from kindergarten feeling tearful and rejected because her classmates had made fun of her. She wanted to be alone in her room, but her mother came in and "grilled her" about her feelings, trying desperately to lift Margie's spirits. When Margie became even more upset, her mother burst into tears herself.

As it turned out, her mother's brother had committed suicide in his twenties and two other family members had received the diagnosis of manic-depressive illness. An underground issue in this family was her mother's fear that she might have passed on the "depression gene" or "suicide gene" to her daughter. It was Margie's job in the family to *not* show depression so as *not* to worry her mother.

When Margie began therapy she was in a polarized arrangement in which her live-in lover was the depressed one. Margie *overfocused* on him and *overfunctioned* for him. She worked in therapy for more than two years to understand the legacy and meaning of "depression" in her own family before she was ready to experiment and slowly share with her mother a bit of her more vulnerable side.

At first, for as long as a year or more, Margie's mother disqualified or minimized Margie's self-disclosures, sometimes changing the topic when Margie shared a small piece of her underfunctioning side. Only gradually did the lines of communication open up around the hot issues of depression and suicide. Even now, four years later, at times of high anxiety Margie's mother will revert to her old pattern ("Just get more sleep and you won't feel sad, honey!") and Margie can gently tease her about it. To an outsider, Margie made "small changes" ("What's the big deal about telling your mother that you had a lousy week?"). For Margie, though, because she was a severe overfunctioner, the change was monumental. This first step helped her to modify her overfunctioning position with her lover and ultimately enlarged her capacity for genuine closeness.

Margie could not have initiated or sustained this change without keeping the long-term process in mind. Nor could she have navigated the change if she had insisted on moving in with a big bang (for example, a heavy confrontation or "deep discussion" with her mother) rather than moving in *slowly* and in *low-key* fashion, counting on countermoves that were as sure as the sunrise.

Resistance from Within

In Kimberly's case, she opted for cutoff, *in part because she really did not want to process the issue of her lesbianism.* Her resistance was quite normal and was manifested by her decision to "orphan herself" after receiving the birthday card signed, "Love, Mom and Dad." Considering the context, this card was a small but significant move *toward connectedness* by her parents—to which Kimberly responded with anger and more distance. *That was Kimberly's countermove to change.*

Processing a loaded issue is not easy. Not only must we define our own position clearly over time, which in Kimberly's case would include some sharing of both the joys and the hardships of being gay, but we must also listen to the *other* person's reaction *without getting too anxious about differences* and without rushing in to change or fix things. It means keeping our own reactivity in check.

When Kimberly finally *did* begin to process the issue with her mother, she found it hard to sit still through her mother's expressions of disappointment and pain. On the one hand, her mother's reactions were entirely predictable, given the negative attitudes toward homosexuality that her mother had absorbed. And in our mother-focused culture, it was no surprise that Kimberly's mother was waking up in the middle of the night obsessed with worry that she had "caused" her daughter's "illness."

But there was more than this. Kimberly's mother also grieved the loss of the unfolding of the generations, as she knew it, as well as the loss of her illusions about her daughter and her images of Kimberly's life. This sudden and forced recognition of profound difference felt to her at first like the severing of her own ties into the future, like the "end of the line," as she put it. That she could identify and express these feelings was ultimately useful. Had she responded only with false liberalism and glib acceptance ("It makes no difference to us that you're gay, honey. We just love you for who you are"), mother and daughter would have lost the opportunity to process the issue before them and to ultimately arrive at a deeper and more authentic dialogue.

Kimberly and her mother could talk together only after Kimberly was able to calmly invite her mother to share her reactions ("Mom, what is the hardest thing for you about my being gay?") and to hear her out over time without becoming critical or defensive. This happened at first through letters, which gave both parties a little more time and space to cool off and think about their own reactions. Only later did Kimberly's mother express an interest in looking through the material that Kimberly had sent her before.

Laying the Groundwork

When Kimberly first revealed her lesbianism, things got off to a particularly difficult start because she opened up the subject in the context of an extremely distant relationship with both her parents. In fact, before D-Day, she almost never discussed personal matters with them. Whether it was good news (organizing a poetry reading at a local university) or bad news (being in a car accident that left her unharmed but badly shaken), Kimberly did not share important information with her family. Distance was the name of the game.

Earlier, I mentioned that you cannot learn to swim by jumping off the high dive. This is particularly true when it comes to emotionally loaded issues. Before bringing up *a big one,* we need to practice bringing up the small ones. And then the medium ones. It may take us several years before we can even picture ourselves in the same room with that other person, talking about the weather.

At Glacial Speed

The more intense the issue and the greater the degree of cutoff, *the more slowly one moves.* For example, many years ago I began working with a woman named Rayna who came to see me because she was unable to enjoy sex with her steady boyfriend. She related the problem to a history of incest which began when she was eleven. More specifically, she had participated in sex play—twice leading to intercourse—with a brother who was seven years her senior.

For the first couple of years in therapy, Rayna worked on processing this incident and putting it in a broader family context. The incest had been one of a number of things that had happened in this family following a traumatic period of multiple losses and an unexplained disappearance in the extended family. Rayna also began reading about incest and attending lectures on it, and she joined a group of incest survivors. During the third year of our work together, Rayna was able to make some initial contact with this brother, starting with sending a Christmas card and later birthday cards to his children. A year later, she stopped briefly at her brother's home for lunch during a cross-country trip and spent two hours with him. A splitting headache preceded the visit, however, and severe back spasms followed it—perhaps signals from Rayna's unconscious that she was attempting too much too soon.

To make a long story short, it was many years before Rayna had established enough contact with her brother to open up and process the issue of incest. Rayna first wrote him a note saying that she had been thinking of many painful events that had happened in their family when she was young, including some between the two of them, and she wanted to talk with him about this at some point. Later, she sat down with him and brought up the subject directly. How did he understand that such a thing could happen in their family? Why did he think it had occurred? How did he make sense of it? Did he still think about it? How had it affected him?

Rayna had prepared herself for the worst-case scenario ("He could deny it and tell me I'm crazy") and had thought about how she would handle this if it occurred—which it didn't. Finally, she clearly let her brother know that she still struggled with this part of her past. She shared that she had been in therapy for years, trying to work through what had happened, and she told him that the incest continued to diminish her self-esteem and influence her relationships with men.

Later on, Rayna and her brother were able to talk about their family and the broader, troubled context in which the incest occurred. At the same time, Rayna did not back down from the matter of individual responsibility. When her brother said, "Well, you didn't stop me," Rayna told him how she saw it. "Look," she said, "I've struggled with terrible guilt about this and I've blamed myself for many years. But I did not initiate sex—and I was eleven and you were eighteen. To me, that is an important difference. I no longer accept the verdict of guilty, although I still struggle with the feelings." In a later letter she elaborated:

> I know that what happened between us did not occur in a vacuum. I've given lots of thought to the things that were happening in our family when the incest began. I've also given lots of thought to what men learn in our society, and how they are taught to dominate women and see women as existing *for* them, sexually and otherwise. I know this is all part of the picture. But I want to be very clear with you that I believe you were responsible for your own actions. If I deny this, or try to deny the anger that I still feel toward you, it will be all the harder for me to work on having a relationship with you. And as painful as it is to try to work this through, it would ultimately be more painful for me to pretend that I don't have a brother.

If the incest had been perpetuated by Rayna's father, the anxiety would have been greater still and Rayna would have moved even more slowly, allowing more time to process the trauma in therapy and understand its occurrence within the larger family context. *Moving at glacial speed* in the face of very high anxiety is the optimal way to proceed. Rather than signifying a lack of strength or perseverance, moving slowly—or sometimes not moving at all—may be necessary to preserving and protecting the well-being and integrity of the self.

Back to the Source

Is it really necessary or even helpful to process a traumatic event or a loaded issue at the source? Why can't we work it all through in a safe and supportive environment such as that provided by therapy or a woman's group? These are places to begin—and many of us will end there too. The gains can be considerable. *I believe, however, that in the long run we will do better if we can move slowly toward some carefully planned contact and eventually unearth the issue with the other person who was directly involved.* The next generations, our children and grandchildren, will also reap the gains.

Processing an issue at the source is important with deceased family members as well. My friend Dorothy lost her father when she was eight, and he was remembered in the family as a superhero. She pictured him on the big screen, full color, with all the imperfections air-brushed out. The actual men in her life were inevitably disappointing because they couldn't fill her father's proverbial big shoes. Two years ago, Dorothy began connecting with her aunt and uncles on her father's side, and she has worked to get a more balanced, objective view of her dad's strengths and weaknesses. The many stories she has gathered, as well as the facts she has learned about his history, have challenged her to think about her father as a real person rather than a cardboard figure defined by family myths and Dorothy's own unconscious wishes and projections. Her contact with her dad's family has been difficult to sustain because it evokes her father's memory for everyone. But being in touch allows Dorothy to stay emotionally connected to her dad and to continue the grieving process in an ultimately productive way.

To the extent that it is possible for us to move slowly *toward,* rather than away from, the emotional issues in our family, we move toward a more solid self and a more objective perspective on others. When painful things have happened and intensity has been managed by distance and cutoff, the "slowly" is especially important because we need first to establish some viable connectedness with family members before trying to bring up a difficult subject.

What Rayna did is not possible for everyone. Even with professional help this may never become a realistic or desirable project for some of us. Ultimately, we each must judge this for our self and trust that we are the best judge of what we can handle. And as always, it's best not to do anything until *after* we have worked to get our own reactivity down.

Down with Reactivity—Up with Thinking

Making disclosures about the self (as Kimberly and Margie did) is not as "hot" as confronting another family member on an intense and taboo subject such as incest. From Kimberly's perspective, however, sharing her lesbianism was loaded enough. Yet prior to her self-disclosure, she put no effort into establishing more connectedness with her folks. Kimberly had talked at length with her friends about coming out, but when the spirit moved her she acted impulsively, without considering her various options (such as timing) or planning how she would handle the strong reactions that her self-disclosure would evoke.

Considering Questions

Part of my job was to help Kimberly *think about* her dilemma rather than *react to it*. Therapists often use *questioning* not only to gather information and to generate and refine hypotheses about the meanings of behavior, but also to foster ability to examine a problem in context, to help lower reactivity, and ultimately to generate new options for behavior. Here is a brief sample of questions that were useful for Kimberly:

When did Kimberly start calling herself a lesbian and what did the word mean to her, then and now? What meanings did she think the word "lesbian" had for each member of her family? How long did it take her to accept her own lesbian identity, and how long would it take family members—more or less? Who in the family did she anticipate would have the strongest negative reaction to the news? Who might accept her lesbian identity most quickly? Most slowly?

Had anyone in her nuclear and extended families ever revealed "a secret," and if so, how had it been received? Was any person on her family tree ever excluded or "denied membership" because of differences? Had Kimberly's family ever been excluded by the community? Were there any cut-offs on her family tree, and if so, what were the circumstances in which these occurred?

How did Kimberly decide to come out at the particular time that she did? Did she think the reaction might have been different if she had approached her parents a year earlier? A year later? Had Mary not been with her at the time, would her parents have listened more or less? How did she anticipate that coming out would alter her relationship with family members, both in the short run and in the long run? How had coming out influenced her relationship with Mary? What factors had influenced Kimberly's willingness, or lack of willingness, to remain invisible as a couple?

This sampling illustrates the kind of questions that ultimately elicit thinking rather than reactivity. Although it's not easy, we can learn to generate questions for ourselves and for others. *Questions enlarge our capacity for reflection and for seeing a problem in its broader context.* This allows us to move back more calmly into an anxiety-filled setting and to continue to process an issue with a more centered focus on the self.

A Matter of Timing

As Kimberly adopted a more reflective attitude, she made a connection between her sister's upcoming marriage and her own intensely felt need to hop on the plane with her lover and let the truth be known. Kimberly opened up an emotionally laden issue in the intense emotional field surrounding her sister's wedding, thus ensuring increased reactivity—her own included.

What specifically was the connection between the upcoming wedding and Kimberly's anxious need for self-revelation? "Competition, I guess," was Kimberly's honest response. "Maybe I was having trouble with the fact that the wedding was all anyone was talking about." Kimberly now appeared to be down on herself, and she spoke as if she were making a fairly heavy confession: "It was 'the wedding this, the wedding that'—everything was the wedding, the wedding, the wedding."

Kimberly's feelings were entirely normal. Feeling jealous and competitive, especially toward those we are close to, is simply a fact of emotional life. Kimberly's feelings were not the problem. The problem was her inability to recognize her feelings (and the associated anxiety), leading to her reactive decision to hop on the plane with Mary. She approached her parents with a heightened need to receive the affirmation that was being showered on her sister, which left her overfocused on getting a particular response from her parents and underfocused on the self.

When we define a new position in a relationship, we need to focus on what we want to say about the self and for the self. We need to be much less focused on the other person's reaction or countermove or on gaining a positive response. This is a goal we achieve *only more or less,* but Kimberly had not laid the groundwork necessary to achieve it more.

Using Feelings as a Guide

Kimberly found it painful to get in touch with her "sibling rivalry" and, perhaps more to the point, her anger toward a world that affirms, honors, and celebrates heterosexual marriage yet fails to recognize or legitimize lesbian bonding. It was only natural that her sister's wedding, which was done up in grand style, would elicit such feelings. But Kimberly's decision to *not* attend the wedding (which she rationalized on financial grounds) only consolidated her outside position in the family and solved nothing in the long run. Later on, Kimberly was able to write both her parents and her sister to apologize for not being with the family on this important occasion. To her sister, she explained that her own pain about having a closeted and uncelebrated partnership might have clouded her thinking. Her apology was much appreciated. At the risk of stating the obvious, I might add that learning to say "I'm sorry" goes a long way toward lowering intensity and shifting a pattern in *any* relationship.

The "negative feelings" that Kimberly at first wished to disavow, later became her guide and incentive for establishing an important marker in her life. She and Mary created their own formal ritual to affirm and celebrate their bond to each other in the presence of their community and before loving witnesses. Her parents and sister, although invited, chose not to attend.

No family member is yet at the level of acceptance where Kimberly would wish them to be. Both her mother and father tell her that they will never accept her sexuality and life-style as "normal." But there are no cutoffs and the lines of communication are reasonably open. Kimberly and

Mary are invited as a couple to family gatherings, and Kimberly's relatives know that Mary is her lifelong partner and not her best friend. Some families might take a decade to reach even this point. In others, this moderate degree of acceptance might not be achievable in a lifetime.

Coming Out or Staying In?

How do you react to Kimberly's story? Some of us will see her choice to come out as an act of great dignity and courage. Others may view it as an immature and selfish act that unnecessarily burdened her family. What do you think?

You don't have to be lesbian to appreciate that the costs of coming out can be very high. On the other hand, the cost of "staying in" may be no less dear, simply less obvious. No sudden and dramatic act of rejection or persecution occurs. One is not suddenly fired from a job, betrayed by a trusted friend, disowned by one's family, or taken to court over custody of one's child. And yet the costs, although harder to identify and easier to deny, may be no less insidious. Failing to come out—although it may be a necessary choice—may feed back a sense of dishonesty, deceit, and self-doubt that erodes one's self-esteem and encourages self-hate. Failing to come out affects the very fabric of relationships and the quality of our day-to-day life. Neither intimacy nor self can flourish in an atmosphere of secrecy and silence.

The question of coming out is not specific only to lesbianism, although those of us who are gay are uniquely vulnerable to discrimination and isolation. Rather, the theme of coming out runs continually through all our lives. Each of us must struggle, both consciously and unconsciously, with our wish to be true to our selves, both privately and publicly, and our wish to receive love, approval, validation, belongingness —or an inheritance, for that matter. It is a struggle we never entirely resolve but one we can work on—in our own way and at our own pace—in a variety of contexts and throughout our lives.

Moving on to Triangles

When we think about intimacy (or the lack of it), we tend to think in terms of *dyads;* that is, two-party interactions. There *are* no key relationships, however, where two people relate to each other uninfluenced and unencumbered by other relationship issues involving a third party. A "pure" person-to-person relationship is only an ideal.

It's an important ideal, at that. If, for example, Kimberly's mother is trying to talk openly with her daughter about lesbianism, one might hope that unresolved issues from her marriage, or from her relationship with her own mother, won't exert a powerful unconscious influence on the process. One might also hope that Kimberly and her mother can work to resolve their own issues relatively free from the influence of others who jump on the bandwagon (Kimberly's sister starts lecturing their mother on how she could handle Kimberly; Mary angrily tells Kimberly that if she's not totally accepted by Kimberly's parents, she won't step foot in their house again). Finally, one might hope that relationship issues would remain in the relationship where they belong rather than being detoured via a third party (if Kimberly's mother fears her mother or husband blame her for Kimberly's lesbianism, she will discuss the issue directly with these parties rather than getting more reactive to Kimberly).

One might *hope* for all of the above, but it's not how we operate. As we will see, the *triangle,* not the dyad, is the basic unit of human emotional functioning, especially under stress.

10

Tackling Triangles

What do you think of when you hear the word "triangle"? For most of us, the "eternal triangle," or extramarital affair, comes right to mind. Affairs are certainly one common form that triangles take in both heterosexual and lesbian couples. Adrienne and Frank's marriage (Chapter 5), for example, was a typical example of how triangles—in this case, his affair, and her affair of the mind—detour marital issues via third parties. An affair may calm the person who is experiencing the most anxiety or discontent and stabilize the marriage until the secret comes out.

After the secret is revealed, relationship issues may still be obscured because so much emotional focus is on the breach of trust that it is difficult for each partner to examine her or his part in the marital distance that predated the affair. The one *having* the affair—in this case, the man—may have difficulty taking appropriate responsibility ("She was so overinvolved with the kids and so sexually rejecting that I found someone who made me feel attractive"). The "done-in" partner may stay so riveted on the betrayal that she never reaches the point where she can get self-focused and work on her own issues. Or she may detour a large percentage of her rage toward the "other woman," which is not where the more serious betrayal occurred.

Because triangles are a natural response to anxiety, affairs often begin at stressful times or important anniversary dates. *He* begins an affair shortly after his dad's stroke or right as his wife approaches her thirty-second birthday, the age when his mother left the family. *She* begins an affair when her firstborn son reaches eleven, which was the age that her older brother was diagnosed with a brain tumor. When we don't find a way to work on anniversaries with our conscious mind, the unconscious will do it for us. Of course, affairs are only one kind of triangle. As we will see, human systems have endless possibilities for triangles and we are always in them.

A Look at an In-Law Triangle

"When I married Rob," Julie explained to me, "we should have moved at least halfway around the world from his mother, Shirley." Julie went on to describe Shirley as the world's most impossible mother-in-law, an intrusive and demanding woman who went from bad to worse after "losing" her only son to marriage. Shirley insisted that Rob and Julie spend every Christmas and Thanksgiving at her home. On weekends, she invariably needed Rob's help with gardening and household chores. Both Julie and Rob described his mother as a woman who simply would not take "No" for an answer.

Within a year after Julie and Rob's wedding, all the negative intensity came to rest between Julie and her mother-in-law. The two women could hardly stand each other, although each got along fine with Rob, who made exhaustive and ineffective efforts to help the two women in his life see each other's point of view. Julie criticized Shirley constantly to Rob ("Your mother is the most demanding, manipulative person I've ever met!")—and to anyone else who would listen. Shirley refrained from openly criticizing her daughter-in-law to Rob, but her negative feelings were obvious.

This is a typical "in-law triangle." The relationship between Rob and his mother—*where the real issues are*—can stay calm, because the intensity has been detoured via Julie and his mother. In fact, Rob doesn't even *recognize* his anger at his mother, because he is so busy coming to her defense in response to his wife's criticism. The triangle allows Rob and his mother to avoid having to navigate a comfortable balance of separateness and connectedness in their own relationship.

In addition, *marital issues are obscured,* as Julie fails to address her own concern about Rob's loyalty to her and *his* problem with setting limits and boundaries around their marriage. She blames his mother ("That woman acts like she's going to have a coronary if she's excluded from anything!") rather than confronting Rob firmly and consistently ("Rob, the repairs have gone unfinished for two weeks and I'd really like you to work on that job before you do your mother's garden"). This way Julie avoids the challenge of taking a clear position with her husband about her own wishes and expectations. Thus, she avoids testing out how Rob would ultimately navigate his loyalty struggle between his mother and wife—and what *she* would do then.

Also fueling the triangle is Julie's distance from her own family of origin, whom she had hoped to "escape" through

marriage and with whom she maintains only dutiful and superficial contact. Because Julie is not attending to issues in
her own family of origin (we *all* have them with family
members—living or dead), she more easily becomes overfocused and overreactive to Rob's mother.

The triangle composed of Julie, Rob, and her mother-
in-law looks like this. Two sides of the triangle remain relatively free of conflict while the negative intensity resides
between Julie and Shirley (Diagram A).

Diagram A

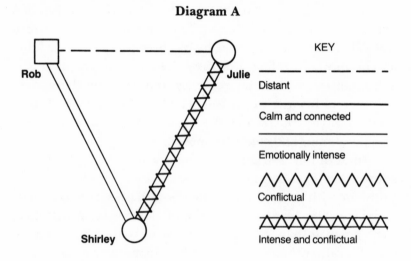

KEY

— — — — — —
Distant

————————
Calm and connected

————————
Emotionally intense

∧∧∧∧∧∧∧∧∧
Conflictual

⟁⟁⟁⟁⟁⟁⟁⟁
Intense and conflictual

Enter, a Child!

Once little Emma came along, other triangles were set
in motion. In response to the anxieties of new fatherhood,
Rob withdrew further into work. To compensate for the lack
of marital intimacy and for her outside position with her
husband and mother-in-law, Julie moved toward forming an
"especially close" relationship with her daughter. The trian-

gle between mother, father, and daughter looked like diagram B:

Diagram B

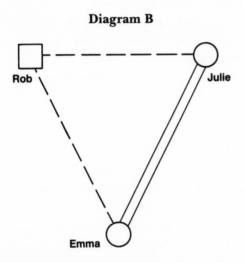

Emma was also an active participant in this triangle. She grew up sensing that her mother needed to be the "number-one parent" and that her dad was made uncomfortable by her emotional presence. Like many daughters, she had a radarlike sensitivity to the distance in her parents' marriage and to her mother's unhappiness. In time, she volunteered to be her mother's ally and "best friend," perhaps as an attempt to fill up her mother's empty bucket and to deflect attention from marital complaints. Even as a toddler, Emma began to put more energy into being "for mother" than into being for her self.

Sex-role pressures also played a major role in the drama of this all-too-familiar triangle. True to stereotype, Julie lacked personal goals and a life plan of her own, which led her to turn to Emma as a "career" rather than a relationship.

Rob became increasingly distant and work-oriented, reinforcing his odd-man-out position in the family.

Over time, each side of the triangle reinforced and maintained the other two sides. The more distant and emotionally isolated Rob became in the family, the more the emotional intensity and intimacy resided between mother and child. And the more Julie and Emma tightened their emotional bond, the more entrenched became Rob's distant position.

A Third Triangle

In time, a third triangle developed, involving Julie, Shirley, and Emma. Shirley began to openly criticize Julie's mothering, even in front of Emma ("You just can't let her go out dressed like that in this cold weather!") and to undermine her authority ("Emma, let's not tell Mommy that I took you for this hot fudge sundae, because she just wouldn't understand"). When anxiety was up, Julie and Shirley would have tense exchanges in front of Emma about her care, and later Julie would blame her husband for not defending her. Rob did everything possible to maintain his distant position in the triangle. It afforded him much relief to be outside the intensity and to be protected from navigating the real emotional issues with his wife, his mother, and his daughter.

If you're feeling a bit lost in these triangles, that's understandable. It's difficult to "think triangles," and even more so when we are in them. Although triangles are difficult to observe, we *all* participate in multiple interlocking triangles, one or two of which are particularly central in our emotional life. Our position in one triangle may be a transient reaction to stress. In another triangle, our position may be rigid, fixed, and highly resistant to change. Triangles solve a problem by lowering anxiety when it can no longer be contained between two persons. But triangles also create a problem by covering up the real relationship issues between any two of the parties and by operating at someone's expense.

Doing Something Different

What if Julie were able to shift her position in one of these stuck triangles? For example, what if she found a way to relate to her mother-in-law calmly and cordially and even stopped criticizing her to Rob? What if Julie also ceased fighting with her mother-in-law about Emma's care and found a way to lower her reactivity in this arena? For example, she might joke with her mother-in-law when Shirley criticized her parenting, instead of fighting with her about it: "Do you really think I'm raising Emma to be a stringbean? [*Laughing*] Well, we Hendersons [*her family name*] have so many pumpkins on our family tree, we could sure use a few stringbeans!" If Julie were feeling particularly courageous about trying out new moves, she might further shift her position in the triangle by asking Shirley to share her expertise, experience, and advice. That is, she could try to relate to Shirley's *competence*, which she has entirely lost sight of.

If Julie could maintain this new position over time, family relationships would shift. Tension and conflict would begin to surface between Rob and his mother. The issues in her own marriage with Rob would also become more clearly identifiable. The triangle might begin to look like diagram C (see page 150).

This would be a transitional stage on the way to more functional relationships. When intensity is up, mother-son

Diagram C

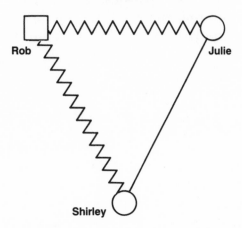

and marital struggles would erupt, offering an opportunity for issues to be identified and addressed where they really are. In addition, Emma would benefit enormously from no longer being the focus of negative intensity between her mother and grandmother. She would have a much easier time growing up.

Of course, to initiate such a change, Julie would need to become more self-focused. She would have to put her primary energy into working on her *own* family rather than on reacting to Rob's. She would also need the courage to sit with the anxiety that is inevitably evoked when we change our part in a key triangle—and the real issues between parties begin to emerge. As we will see in the next chapter, changing our part in a stuck triangle is anything but easy.

Why is it Julie's job to change the triangle? It's not. Nor did Julie *make* the triangle happen. Each person in a triangle is responsible for their own behavior and any one person can change his or her own steps. The triangles that we get *most* stuck in are at least several generations in the making and their major ingredient is chronic anxiety. No one person "does it" to the other two.

As usual, the person who is concerned or in the most pain is often the one who finds the will to change. Rob could also change the triangle, but he is unlikely to do so because he is more comfortable with the status quo. The triangle protects him from facing the real emotional issues in his relationships with his mother, his wife, and his daughter.

So, What Is a Triangle?

Do you recall how anxiety can affect a relationship system? People divide into two camps, one or both parties get overfocused on the other (and underfocused on the self) in a blaming or worried way, and they ultimately wind up in extreme and polarized positions.

There is, however, an additional part to the story. *Two-person systems are inherently unstable. Anxiety and conflict will not stay contained between two parties for more than a short time.* A third party will quickly be triangled in (or will triangle him- or herself in). This process operates automatically, like a law of physics, without conscious awareness or intent.

The third party in a triangle may be in one person's camp at the expense of a relationship to the other (you don't see your Uncle Joe since your mother stopped speaking to him; you are cut off from your dad since he divorced your mother). The third party may be in a mediating, peace-making, or fix-it position (your parents fight and you move in to advise the parent with whom you have the most influence). Or the original two parties may get focused on a third individual, in a worrying or blaming way (as marital distance increases or an important anniversary date approaches, you and your husband become increasingly anxious about a child; you and your dad talk frequently about your mother's depression, convinced that you both know what's best for her).

Triangles take countless forms, but we can count on the fact that when tensions rise between two parties, a third will be triangled in, lowering anxiety in the original pair. The third party may be *inside* the family (a child, stepmother, grandparent, or in-law)—or *outside* the family (an affair or best friend). Even a therapist can be a third leg in a triangle if he or she joins the client's camp at the expense of a spouse or other family member. Such triangulation can also occur if a therapist is fostering a "special" close relationship that detours intensity from real relationships rather than increasing the client's motivation to solve emotional issues at their source.

A Word About Gossip

Gossip is a universal form of triangling with which we are all familiar. The higher the underground anxiety between two parties, the more the conversation will focus on a third. For example, when you meet your mother for lunch, a big chunk of the conversation may be about your dad, or the problems of your younger brother. There may be little real sharing of self by either you or your mom that doesn't involve a worried (or blaming) focus on someone else.

You can just about measure the level of anxiety in a work system or family system by the amount of gossip. By "gossip," I mean talk *about* another person, with a focus on that person's incompetence or "pathology." We consolidate our relationship with one party at the expense of a third—or we attempt to dilute our anxiety by getting others in our camp. Gossip has nothing to do with intentions. Our conscious intentions may be only the best.

A friend of mine returned from a Christmas dinner with her extended family where the underground anxiety had been quite high. This Christmas was the first without her maternal grandparents, who had both died during the past year. "It was a zoo!" my friend exclaimed upon her return home. "My aunt was cornering me to tell me how my mother is not taking care of her appearance; my mother was angry at her brother and didn't want me to sit next to him; my father cornered me to tell me in hushed tones about my mother's crying spells . . . and so it went!" No one talked about the missing grandparents and how sad the family was that they were not there.

Does talking about a third party *always* indicate a triangle? Of course not. For example, we may have a problem with a friend or co-worker and approach a third party for support or to obtain a more objective perspective. This kind of discussion may allow us to calm down and consider new options for dealing with the original party. Often, however, we have the best intentions for talking *about* a particular individual ("I just want my daughter to know the truth about her father!") when actually we are inviting someone into our camp and operating at the other party's expense. This is particularly true if the person we are talking to (e.g., our daughter) needs to have a relationship with the person we are talking *about* (e.g., her father).

If dyads are inherently unstable, triangles are inherently stable, just as a tricycle is more stable (although less functional) than a two-wheeler. Triangles can last for years, for decades, and over generations. They are not "wrong," "bad," or "sick," but rather are natural ways to manage anxiety in human systems. They serve the adaptive function of stabilizing relationships and lowering anxiety when it can no longer be contained between two parties. Triangles are simply the basic unit of human emotional functioning. As with any relationship pattern, the question is how flexible or fixed is the process?

Child-Focused Triangles

Children are ready-made for triangles; they absorb and detour anxiety from any source. Let's look briefly at a typical child-focused triangle that was a relatively *transient* reaction to anxiety and stress.

"For Willy's Sake"

Bill, a thirty-seven-year-old high school principal, became anxious when his wife, Sue, was accepted into a doctoral program in counseling psychology. Like many men, he was unable to articulate his fears directly, even to himself. Instead, he worried about the well-being of their two-year-old son, and confronted his wife on the child's behalf: "Willy needs you at home! I won't have him raised by a stranger!"

As Bill and Sue argued about "Willy's needs," their son became more anxious and began to react loudly to his mother's departures. A vicious cycle ensued as Bill intensified both his concern about his son and his criticism of his wife ("You see how sensitive he is to your absence!"). Willy, in turn, became even more ill-behaved and clingy.

It took only a few months of nonproductive fighting and blaming for both Bill and Sue to become self-focused and to address the issues between them. Sue, a black woman, was the first person in her family to enter a doctoral program; she had more than her fair share of anxiety, which she avoided by fighting with Bill. Bill got in touch with how threatened he felt about Sue's graduate studies, and with his discomfort at his own father's criticism of Sue's decision.

With a little help, Bill was able to articulate his fears to Sue and to talk directly with his dad about his disapproving attitude. Sue got in touch with her own discomfort about her pioneering position in her family, including her anxiety and guilt about having opportunities that were not available to previous generations of women, or men, in her family. She was able to talk with her mother, sister, and grandmother about her fear of both success and failure, and so learned more about their reactions to her decision to pursue a doctorate.

As Bill and Sue began to work on their *own* issues, little Willy stopped acting out. No longer the focus of parental anxiety, he was also less afraid that something bad would happen between his parents if his mother went back to school. Within a few months, the entire family had calmed down enough to weather Sue's transition to graduate student with a minimum of stress. Although this couple was unusually quick to get unstuck from a child-focused process, their situation illustrates that it can be done.

A Societal Triangle

This child-focused triangle is also evident at the *societal level*. Think back to the initial male response to the women's movement. Men did *not* typically say, "I'm scared and threatened by the changes women are making." Or, "I don't *want* to share housework and child care, and so I feel resentful when my wife asks me to do so." At the early stages of feminism, we did not often hear men speak about the self, or in "I" language, or with their own voice.

Instead, the media focused relentlessly on "the needs of children," which pulled everyone's heartstrings. In the '70s we all were treated to the picture of the small child staring glassy-eyed at the institutional walls of the day care center— while his mother ran off to fulfill her potential. The image itself was enough to frighten and induce guilt in any would-be feminist, and then *Kramer vs. Kramer* became a big hit. This "Change back!" reaction was a countermove to women's efforts to define the self, and not surprisingly, it took the form of blaming women and focusing on children.

Of course children have needs. But so do mothers and fathers. This focus on "the needs of children" did not reflect an *actual* investment in supporting the many children and families who needed help. Rather, it was a typical societal triangle, similar to the one between Bill, Sue, and Willy. Focusing on "the needs of children" ("Mama stay home!") protected us from identifying the locus of the problem's existence—*between* grown men and women. How *easy* it was to express worry that children would be damaged by misguided women in flight from their maternal responsibilities. How *difficult* it was (and still is!) for men and women to *work together* in order to change policy, work institutions, and family roles so that we can be a nurturant and cooperative society *truly* attentive to the needs of children and families!

Whenever adults are not actively working to identify and solve their own problems, then the focus on children

may be especially intense or children may volunteer to deflect, detour, and act out adult issues in most imaginative
ways. Indeed, children tend to inherit *whatever* psychological
business we choose not to attend to.

A good friend tells the story of becoming extremely
reactive after a teacher's conference in which she was told
that her second-grader might be an "underachiever." She
began to monitor her daughter closely, looking for any evi-
dence of a problem; her daughter, in turn, became more
anxious. Several weeks later, as my friend found herself lecturing this seven-year-old child on "goal setting," she suddenly realized that she herself had been feeling particularly
stuck regarding her *own* professional directions. She had
recently arrived at an important anniversary date, the age
when her own mother—a bright and colorful woman—took
a downhill turn and became increasingly unable to use her
own competence. With this greater degree of self-focus, my
friend was able to apologize matter-of-factly to her daughter
for being on her back and explain that the issue was really
her own. As she put her energies into working on it, her
daughter's anxiety lessened.

Rampant Reactivity:
From Child-Focus to Self-Focus

Child-focused triangles can be extraordinarily intense, depending on the level of anxiety fueling them. Consider this
firsthand report.

Several years ago, my family went out to dinner and
then to a Saturday night baseball game in Kansas City. At the
restaurant, I found myself concerned about my son
Matthew's sluggishness and apparent fatigue. Later I no-

ticed that he got up to go to the restroom four times during the game: he looked sick to me. Shortly before the ninth inning, I suddenly "knew" in my bones that Matthew (then age ten) had juvenile diabetes. The idea hit me not as just a possibility or a concern, but as a dreadful and unbearable truth.

My husband, Steve, often minimizes his concern in proportion to my exaggerated position, but not that night. By the time we got home that evening, Steve was well into the marital fusion and he was scared too. He called the pediatrician early Sunday and described the symptoms (fatigue and constant urination) that we had observed in Matthew the night before. The pediatrician suggested we wake Matthew immediately and meet him at the hospital emergency room. In retrospect, I imagine that the doctor's own sense of urgency (he might simply have told us to watch Matthew that day and get back to him) was partly a response to our contagious anxiety.

Steve woke Matthew and explained the terrible situation with as much calm as he could muster. With a heavy heart, I watched them head off to the hospital. I stayed home with our younger son, Ben, so unable to contain my own anxiety that I called my friend Emily to stay with me during the waiting period. I have faced far more potentially serious crises than juvenile diabetes in my lifetime, but I have never experienced anything worse than that Sunday morning. Until I received the report that Matt's blood test was normal, I could hardly stay within my own skin.

Obviously, my emotional reaction far exceeded even the reality of juvenile diabetes, had this unlikely diagnosis been confirmed. Later, I felt terrible about what I had dumped on Matthew, who was understandably shaken by being the focus of such extreme intensity.

Back to Self-Focus

The emotional process in my family on that particular weekend was as intense and dysfunctional as one could find in any family on this planet. If anxiety gets high enough, none of us is immune from going off the deep end with however we manage anxiety—be it overfunctioning, underfunctioning, distancing, fighting, or child-focus. Significantly, however, I did not stay *stuck* in reactive gear; that's what makes the difference. I hope I would not have stayed too long in the reactive gear even if the diagnosis had been different.

Once I was able to call on the *thinking* part of my brain (which took time and help from my friends), it was evident I had my work cut out for me. I needed to get a clearer perspective on my own health anxieties—anxieties that have roots in issues and events that have come down over many generations. I thought I had "dealt with all that," because I had had several weighty conversations with family members about my mother's first cancer and my grandmother's early death from tuberculosis. Of course, it's a *process,* and working through the emotionally loaded issues on our family tree may take several lifetimes. Working on them *consciously*—even a little bit—offers many advantages over letting the unconscious do it for us.

And so I was on the phone again with my mother and sister, asking questions about the legacy of health issues and "worry" on our family tree. I felt somewhat chagrined by my failure to connect my worry about Matthew to my own misdiagnosis with diabetes years earlier. And only two weeks before the ball game, a routine physical had revealed sugar in my urine. I had seen an endocrinologist, who diagnosed my condition as glucose intolerance.

Another obvious factor (which I had not thought about) was that my mother's diagnoses of cancer and diabetes had occurred the same year and were thus mixed up in my mind, just as I was prone (as are we all) to mixing myself up with my mother—and with my children. And when I took out my genogram (family tree) to study a bit more, I also realized why diabetes was a loaded issue for me and why "survival" anxieties had surfaced during this particular month. The details of my family history are only important here in that they enabled me to put my emotional energy back into my own issues. We all have important emotional issues—and if we don't process them *up* the generations, we are more than likely to pass them on *down*.

A Familiar Lesson

Kids aside, we are always in triangles of one sort or another because we always have "stuff" from our first family (as well as elsewhere) that we are not paying attention to and that may overload other relationships. Throughout this book, we have examined how we detour anxiety and emotionality from one relationship to another. Seeing the process in our own lives, however, is no easy matter, and working on it is even harder.

Working on triangles means more than identifying and addressing issues with our first family that fuel anxiety elsewhere. It also means observing and modifying our current role in key family triangles. Sometimes a triangle will last only a day, a week, or several months, as the examples in this chapter illustrate. But any relationship pattern can become chronically stuck if we don't become calm enough to examine our part in it.

Let's look now at an entrenched family triangle where anxiety was chronically high and where an underfunctioning-overfunctioning polarity had been in high gear for as long as anyone could remember. We'll also think a bit more about our own position in triangles, which should help us further understand the fine points of the overfunctioning-underfunctioning dance.

11

Bold New Moves: The Story of Linda

Linda, a twenty-eight-year-old financial planner, came to see me with the goal of working on her "poor judgment with men." One week after her first appointment, however, a family crisis placed another matter at the top of the agenda. Her younger sister, Claire, was acting depressed and, according to her mother, was leaving her apartment a mess and eating poorly. Both parents responded with intense anxiety, scooping Claire up and taking her back to stay with them in their small nearby apartment. There they cooked for her, did her laundry, and set her up with a therapist whom Claire refused to see after three appointments.

Linda herself was anxious about her sister, who fourteen months earlier had been hinting that she was considering suicide. At the same time, however, Linda was angry with her parents, especially her mother, whom she blamed for her sister's problems. "My mother has never let Claire grow up, *that's* the problem!"

During anxious times such as this one, Linda dispensed copious advice to her mother about how to manage Claire, which her mother ignored. Linda, in frustration and anger, would then seek distance from her entire family. "The best thing I can do for my own mental health," she stated flatly during our early work together, "is to stay as far away from that crazy group of people as possible!"

So, What's Wrong Here?

Linda began therapy with the notion that telling other family members what they were doing wrong (or not doing right) was the hallmark of assertiveness and selfhood. As we have seen, however, this belief is hardly true. *True selfhood and assertiveness are self-focused, not other-focused.*

Linda also thought that her mother made Claire sick. *Mothers cannot make their children sick.* Mothers are only part of a much larger picture and they do not have power over the whole.

In addition, Linda saw herself as having the answers to their family problems, and she blamed her mother for failing to follow her good advice. Linda did not recognize how her own behavior contributed to the problem she was trying to fix.

Finally, Linda thought that the best thing for her own mental health was to distance as much as possible. But that didn't work either. It lowered her anxiety, but only temporarily. Linda began eating excessively, and often awakened early in the morning anxiously preoccupied with the fear that her sister might kill herself.

Tracking the Triangle

What was Linda's position in this common family triangle? When anxiety was low, her relationship with her mother seemed calm and close, although their "closeness" rested heavily on their mutual focus on Claire. Claire, a chronic focus of concern, had the more distant relationship to both her mother and her sister. (See Diagram D.)

Diagram D

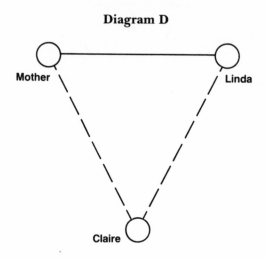

Claire's outside position in the triangle could get quite pronounced as her mother and Linda consolidated their relationship at her expense. For example, her mother would tell Linda "secrets" that were not for Claire's ears, because Claire would get "too upset" or "tell the wrong person." Linda participated in the secret-keeping business at a cost to both Claire and their relationship as sisters. Claire also did her part to maintain her role as the fragile one, or the one who couldn't be counted on.

When anxiety was up, the "inside" positions in the triangle became far less comfortable. Calm gossip turned into angry tension between Linda and her mother, as Linda would tell her mother what to do about Claire and her mother would discount her advice. During one visit home, for example, Linda watched her mother wash and fold two baskets of Claire's laundry, while Claire sat on the living room couch thumbing through magazines. Linda phoned her mother the next day and let her have it. "Claire will never grow up if you keep treating her like a baby! She has arms! She has legs! She's twenty-three years old! She can carry a laundry basket!" Linda's mother, for her part, felt misunderstood and believed that Linda failed to appreciate the gravity of Claire's situation. During the particularly stressful period after Linda began therapy, the triangle looked like this:

Diagram E

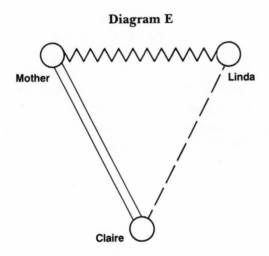

When Linda and her mother talked (or argued) about Claire's problems, both were concerned about her. Surely they did not intend to have a relationship at her expense. As we have seen, however, the patterned ways in which we move under anxiety are rarely helpful. It is simply not helpful to an

underfunctioning individual to overfocus on her (or him)—
or to talk *about* her at the expense of talking *to* her. And
efforts to mediate, make peace, or fix another family relationship are just about doomed to failure. We cannot be
therapists in our own family.

So what *does* help? And how does one begin to move out
of such a triangle in order to create a new dance?

Out of the Middle

Linda's first challenge was to try to *stay out* of the relationship issues between her mother and her sister, and to work
toward having a separate, person-to-person relationship
with each of them. At the beginning of therapy, Linda could
not move in this direction, because *like any good overfunctioner, she was convinced that her mother and sister needed her
help and that she had the answers for them.* For a long time,
Linda clung tenaciously to this view despite her mother and
sister's failure to solve their problems and despite seeing her
advice only temporarily heeded at best.

What exactly would staying out look like to Linda—or
to any of us, for that matter? Staying out does *not* mean that
Linda crosses her arms in front of her chest and announces
firmly to her mother and sister, "Please keep me out of this
triangle! You don't take my advice anyway, and it's not helpful for me to be involved!" Such a position would still reflect
a reactive, "I-really-know-what's-best-for-you" stance. And
it's a blaming and distancing position as well.

Let's look at what staying out actually requires. We will
also learn more about the fine points of overfunctioning,
because learning how *not* to function for other people is a

big chunk of the task at hand. When we *take responsibility for* another person, in contrast to *taking a responsible position in* that relationship, we are operating at that person's expense. Because this notion challenges the worldview of the over-functioning individual, many of us just don't "get it."

As we look at the specific changes that Linda made in her family, try to think about your own relationships. Keep in mind that the specific players and the specific symptoms (for example, Claire's depression) are less important than understanding the patterned ways in which we operate under stress. This triangle could have been with Linda, her mother, and her father; it could have been with Linda, her mother, and her grandmother; or it could have been with Linda and her two best friends. Instead of depression, Claire could have had any other emotional or physical problem. The principles of stuckness and change remain the same.

Getting off Claire

When Linda was ready to work on this core triangle, she began by trying to keep the conversation with her mother focused *less* on Claire and *more* on the two of them. Because core triangles are pretty intense (your mother is off the plane only five minutes before she says, "Let me tell you what your father has done now!"), shifting the focus can be quite a challenge.

Linda handled it pretty well. She stayed nonreactive when her mother talked about Claire, and she did not partic-ipate in diagnostic conversations or offer advice. She shifted the conversation toward *sharing more about herself* ("I've been having a real dilemma at work this week") and *learning more about her mother's family* ("Mom, wasn't Aunt Carole on some kind of medication for depression? Did she ever talk with you about the problem?").

Moving out of the triangle did not mean that Linda flatly refused to talk about Claire, which of course is a distancing position. Linda just didn't get into it in the old way. She still gave her mother occasional feedback when appropriate, but *not in an intense, advice-giving, or instructive way.* Here's an example of her changed behavior, which illustrates this crucial distinction.

One afternoon when Linda and her mother were shopping, her mother's focus on Claire was particularly intense. The situation at home had become unbearable, she said, with Claire just hanging around the house making impossible and manipulative demands. Linda heard her out and then said lightly, "Well, Mom, you're just so competent at doing for others and doling out all that good stuff—it makes sense to me that other people would be more than eager to take all they could get."

In this brief statement, Linda shifted significantly from the old pattern. She gave feedback (that is, by clarifying her own thoughts on an issue) in a light manner, without becoming instructive and without asking her mother to follow her advice. The perspective that she shared did not blame or take sides, but was, rather, a calm reflection on the dance as she saw it (their mother was good at giving, Claire was good at taking). When her mother ignored her comment, Linda did not take it further, recognizing that her mother's anxiety was too high to allow her to absorb even light feedback. Her mother and Claire would either solve their problems together, or they would not.

Getting Put to the Test

Moving out of a triangle is a process that will test us over and over. When we start to move out, others in the triangle will intensify their efforts to invite us back in, which is just human nature and the normal resistance to change. Linda's efforts to shift her position in the triangle with her mother and sister encountered this kind of "Change back!" reaction.

Claire was preparing to leave for a three-day trip to Cape Cod, where she planned to stay with some friends who were renting a summer cottage. At this time, however, she was acting mopey and depressed, and she had commented twice to her parents that life didn't seem worth living. Her mother did not think Claire was fit to go on the trip and tried to convince her to stay home. When this failed, she phoned her daughter's friends to express her concern. She asked them to provide a "low-stress" visit for Claire, to watch her for signs of depression, and to call if they noticed anything that looked "serious." Claire's mother did not tell her about the call, and she asked her daughter's friends to keep the call confidential. On the last day of Claire's visit, however, one of them spilled the beans.

Claire was furious with her mother about the incident, and unconsolable. Mother felt Claire was "overreacting"— blowing things entirely out of proportion. Claire, still living at her parents' home, began refusing meals with them, choosing to eat at a nearby McDonald's instead. At this point, her mother called Linda and implored her to "talk some sense" into her sister. This call provided Linda with an opportunity to practice *not* returning to her old pattern.

Linda rose to the challenge. She told her mother that she really didn't have the slightest idea how to be helpful to the two of them, and she expressed confidence that both parties could work out their difficulties over time. When her mother pressed her, she did not return to her old overfunctioning position, but rather responded empathetically to the struggle facing her mother and sister, indicating that she knew it was not easy. She said, "Mom, it sounds like you and Claire are really at a standoff. I love you both and I'm sorry that this is such a tough time. I know it looks impossible right now, but maybe later on things will look different."

At the same time, Linda did not back down from sharing her perspective when asked. Again, the ability to share our thoughts, values, and beliefs is part of *defining a self. Such sharing is not overfunctioning—if we can do it calmly, with respect for differences (others need not see things our way), and with an understanding that our way may not work for or fit others.*

And so—when asked—Linda let her mother know that she also would have been upset if she had been Claire, because she would have wanted her mother to deal with her directly rather than secretly call her friends. When her mother said, "You mean *you* wouldn't have made the call if you were scared to death about your daughter?!" Linda replied thoughtfully, "Well, if I had made the call, I would have told Claire about it. That's just my way."

When her mother angrily accused her of not understanding that Claire was impossible to talk to directly, Linda didn't argue. Instead, she said lightly, "Well, I'm just sharing my own thoughts about managing a difficult situation. I'm not saying I have the right answers." When her mother added, "And your sister is just trying to make me feel guilty by eating her meals in McDonald's every night!" Linda laughed and said, "I guess I wouldn't be doing things *her* way either. Nothing in the world would get me to eat a Big Mac if your home cooking was on the table!" At this point, her mother laughed too, and the tension eased a bit.

And Again, and Again!

Of course, this was not the last test Linda had to deal with. As we have seen, substantive change is a process that is never quite finished. The following week, the relationship between Claire and her mother escalated to a fever pitch. When Linda dropped by one afternoon to pick up a package, her mother cornered her in the bathroom. As Linda described it, "Mother looked so tense and puffed up that I thought she was about to pop." Mother put her face right up to Linda's and spoke in an angry whisper. "Do you know what your sister is doing now! She has stopped speaking to me! Can you believe that she is behaving this way! What do you think of *that! You* would never do anything like that, would you!?"

At first Linda clutched inside. She felt momentarily panicky, the way Kristen (Chapter 7) did when her dad called her to insist that she drive him home. But then she was able to think. "You know, Mother," Linda reflected, "you're probably right. I don't think I'd handle the situation the way Claire is because that's not my way. I think it would just be too painful for me to be feeling that distant from a family member. But as I've shared with you, I wouldn't have handled the situation your way either." Linda smiled and then added warmly, "I guess it makes sense that I'd handle the situation in my *own* way, since I'm different from both of you."

Her mother looked exasperated and said that she needed to start dinner. When she called Linda later that week, she did not mention Claire. When Linda visited several weeks later, it was obvious that her mother and Claire were sharing the easiest communication Linda had seen in a long time. "I feel kind of humbled by the whole experience," Linda told me later that week in psychotherapy. "They really are doing better without my help." It was Linda's first real experience of staying *calm* and *connected*—yet *outside* the old triangle.

These dialogues were dramatic turning points for Linda, and they came after much hard work in therapy. Yet Linda needs to appreciate that the work she is doing will always be "in progress." Whenever anxiety is high in her family, everyone, including Linda, will tend to reinstate the old pattern. Such is the nature of triangles and human systems. What is important is not that Linda always stay calm and "get it right," which is simply not humanly possible, but that she slowly move forward, and not backward, over time.

Connecting with Claire

As Linda stopped having the answers for other family members, she became more in touch with her *own* worry about her sister, as well as her own distance. Claire had talked suicide long before Linda had started therapy, but Linda had not really asked Claire direct questions or shared her own fears.

Linda was occasionally anxiously preoccupied with the subject, and like a true big sister, she had prescribed everything from exercise and medication to psychoanalysis. But the lines of communication were not really open. When I asked Linda how serious her sister had ever been about suicide (Had Claire ever made a plan?), Linda was not sure. Nor did she know what Claire's *own* perspective was on her depression, what efforts she had made to solve it, and what she had found helpful or not.

And so, Linda made a courageous act of change when she asked her sister *direct questions about suicide* and *shared her own reactions.* She put the issue squarely on the table: "Claire, I may be overreacting, but are you actually thinking about suicide?" When Claire's answer still left Linda feeling vague about the facts ("Well, Tuesday night I was sort of thinking about it, but I think I'm doing better now"), Linda asked questions that demanded more specificity. For example: "Where are you now on a one-to-ten scale, if *one* means that suicide is just a fleeting thought and *ten* means that you have a specific plan you're about to carry out?" "If tomorrow night you had a plan, would you let someone in the family know?"

Given the profound degree of anxiety surrounding a subject such as suicide, questioning may quickly take on a blaming, diagnostic, or overfunctioning tone. Linda was better able to avoid this because she was working in therapy to manage her own anxiety and to maintain a high degree of self-focus. Over time, she had reached a deeper and more genuine recognition that she could not change or fix her sister, or even know what was best for her. Certainly, no family member could keep Claire alive or solve her problems. What Linda *could* do for her sister was to care about her and to keep in touch.

Learning to ask clear questions—to go for the facts—is a skill, as well as a courageous act. If we are concerned that a significant other is in trouble, be it from an eating disorder, AIDS, suicide, drugs, or low grades, for that matter, it is not helpful to avoid asking direct questions. We all have reasons *not* to ask ("I can't do anything anyway," "If I mention drugs, he'll just deny it," "If I say anything, it may just put ideas in her head"). Over the long haul, however, we all tend to do better when we have open lines of communication with our significant others.

Sharing a Reaction

Opening up the lines of communication requires more than becoming a skilled questioner. It also requires sharing our reactions and giving feedback. "I" language is a priority here. Often we think we are *sharing about self,* when actually we are trying to be an expert on the other.

Linda shared her reactions with Claire when she told Claire how shaken she was at the thought of losing her: "Claire, the thought that you might ever try to kill yourself terrifies me. I love you and you're the only sister I have. I can't imagine how I would handle it if you were gone." When Linda finished speaking, she burst into tears. It was the first time in Claire's adult life that she had seen her big sister cry.

These words may seem so *obvious,* or even trite, that you might wonder why they constitute a courageous act of change. Yet the higher the anxiety, the more difficulty an overfunctioner (or distancer) has simply sharing pain, fear, and concern without anger or blame and without having answers or advice for the other person. It's hard to find the right words to say the simplest things: "I don't know how I'd handle it, to lose you in this way. I love you, and I want you to be around for as long as possible. I can't bear the thought that I could lose you now. I know that I can't do a thing to help you solve this problem, but I want you to know how much I care about you."

Setting Limits—Taking a Position

Of course, stepping out of overfunctioning does *not* mean that we fail to set limits and take a position on emotional issues. As we saw with Kristen and her dad, relationships can only become more chaotic and impaired when we cannot clarify limits or do not state clearly what we will and will not do.

What position did Linda ultimately take around the suicide issue? First, she clarified that she would not keep the issue of suicide a secret from any family member. Nor would she aid and abet her sister's self-destructive behavior in any other way. Again, regardless of the nature of the problem, our challenge is to define a clear and responsible position in the relationship, *for self* and not as an attempt to function for the other party. A look at a conversation between these two sisters illustrates how to "take a responsible position for self" and how difficult doing so can be. Such interactions are tough on both parties.

At one point, Linda asked Claire to let her know if she ever felt suicidal, and she expressed her wish for a closer relationship. Linda said she'd like for them both to feel free to call each other when they felt down. Claire immediately challenged this move toward more connectedness.

"Why should I tell you if I'm suicidal?" demanded Claire. "You can't do anything to help me when I'm depressed."

"I know that," Linda answered. "I don't even have the answers to my own problems, let alone yours. But even if I could only give you a hug and tell you I care, I would still like to know."

"Well, you'll have to promise me that you won't tell Mom and Dad. They would just overreact or put me in a hospital or something."

"I can't make you that promise," Linda replied. "I would never keep it a secret if I thought your life was in danger. For one thing, my *own* anxiety would be out of control if I held that kind of secret. I just couldn't do it. Yes, I'd call Mom and Dad. No, I wouldn't keep it a secret from anyone in the family."

"If Mom and Dad were away, would *you* ever put me in the hospital?" Claire asked accusingly.

"Claire, if I thought you might kill yourself . . . I'd call the police, the fireman, the hospital, or whoever I could think of. If you told me you were in immediate danger, I wouldn't know what else to do. I know you'd be furious with me, but I'd just have to live with that. I *couldn't* live with the feeling that I had aided your killing yourself. I just couldn't live with that."

"But you can't stop me anyway if I really want to."

"I know that, Claire. Of course I can't stop you. But as I said, I wouldn't sit around and be part of it happening. I'd be on the phone to everyone who loves you."

"Well then, forget it!" was Claire's quick and angry reply. "I'm not telling you *anything*." Claire left the room then.

Linda sat by herself for about five minutes. Then, before leaving, she told her sister: "Claire, I'm really hoping you'll reconsider what you said about not telling me anything, because I care about you. As your sister, I feel terribly sad to think we could end up not being able to talk about things that are important to us. I've been thinking about Mom and Aunt Sue [*a sister from whom their mother is cut off*] and I think how much I *don't* want us to end up like that."

This conversation illustrates the key aspects of "defining a self" that we have touched on in earlier chapters. Let's summarize:

First, Linda is maintaining a nonreactive position. Emotional, yes. Linda cried when she told Claire she was scared of losing her, and that she felt terrible about the prospect that they might end up as distant as their mother and Aunt Sue. But Linda was *thinking,* and she was maintaining her new position rather than reacting to anxiety in her usual patterned ways.

Second, Linda defined a clear bottom-line position ("No, I won't keep suicide a secret. Yes, I'd call the police or hospital, if necessary") and stood behind it, even in the face of intense emotional pulls to do otherwise. Linda resisted the temptation to back down from her position, and then perhaps to blame her sister for "manipulating" or "blackmailing" her.

Finally, Linda stayed entirely self-focused and stuck with "I" language—nonblaming statements about the self. She put her energy into taking a responsible position in the relationship—and not into taking responsibility *for* her sister, or acting as if she could solve her sister's problem. She did not lapse back into overfunctioning. At no time did Linda suggest that she was a better expert on Claire than Claire was on her self. This was part of a new pattern for Linda where she stayed in her own skin and worked to *relate to her sister's competence*—something we easily forget how to do when we are relating to a chronically underfunctioning individual.

Sharing Underfunctioning

What else did Linda need to do to create a different dance with Claire? Linda slowly shared some of her *own* problems with Claire, as well as with her parents. She started slowly, with small pieces of information, because of the extreme difficulty of modifying overfunctioning. Sharing one's vulnerability with family members and seeing the underfunctioners as having something to offer are not easy shifts.

Thus, Linda did *not* begin by telling her sister about her poor track record in choosing men, which had led her to therapy because she despaired of ever having a decent relationship. Instead, when Claire became depressed and called her one evening, Linda told her she wasn't really able to listen or be helpful right then. "Everything has gone wrong today," Linda complained to her sister. "In fact, I was just about to call you. I messed up a meeting at work, I burned my dinner, and I'm just feeling totally stressed-out." For Linda, this sharing was yet another courageous act of change. It pushed against the polarities in her family, where there was *too much focus* on the incompetence of one member and *not enough focus* on the incompetence of others. Later, when she was ready, she shared with Claire some of her problems with men and openly acknowledged that this was *her* significant area of underfunctioning. She also asked her sister for advice and help in areas where Claire had a history of expertise.

Linda and Men

When Linda first came to see me, her primary concern was her long-standing problem with men. Her relationships tended to intensify quickly, and equally quickly she would lose her ability to be objective about the man she was dating. She described herself as "a leaf blown about by the wind" when it came to romantic involvement—a stark contrast to her usual sense of mastery and control on the job.

Many firstborn, overfunctioning daughters share Linda's experience. And although the connection may seem elusive, the work she did on her own family was particularly helpful. Linda worked to modify her overfunctioning position and to share a more whole and balanced self with her sister and parents, which included *both* her competence and vulnerability. She also worked in therapy to obtain a more objective and balanced view of both the strengths and weaknesses of other family members. *In turn, she began to look more objectively at the men she was dating.* Things still heated up fast, but Linda could then step back to consider the strengths and weaknesses of a prospective mate.

Over time, Linda put much effort into observing and changing her part in some old patterns, polarities, and triangles in her family. In addition to the shifts she made with Claire and her mother, she also connected more with her father, who was an extreme distancer and something of an invisible phantom on the family scene. As Linda learned more about her dad's own family and history and shared more of herself with him, she was also on firmer footing with her male partners. The more we can stay connected and define a clear and whole self in the intense field of family relationships, the more grounded we are in other relationships.

At the time Linda terminated psychotherapy, she was not dating anyone in particular nor did she feel a great need to be. She was, however, doing a fine job of avoiding relationships that would ultimately waste her energy or bring her pain.

A Postscript: The Dilemma of Overfocus

When another person underfunctions—be it a misbehaved child, a depressed husband, a symptomatic sibling—significant others may become focused on that person. Over time, the focus on the other may increase, whether through blaming, worrying, fixing, bailing out, protecting, pulling up slack, covering up, or simply paying too much attention with too much intensity. To the same extent, the focus on self decreases, with less energy going toward identifying and working on one's own relationship issues and clarifying one's own goals and life plan. When this happens, the underfunctioner will only tend to underfunction more and longer.

We cannot simply *decide* to deintensify our reactivity and focus on another person's problems. It's not something we can just "do," nor is it something we can pretend. If we try to fake it, our efforts will be short-lived at best, or we may flip from overfocus to reactive distance—the other side of the same coin. We can deintensify our focus on the other only *after* we find the courage to work on other relationships and issues that we do not want to pay attention to. Each of us has enough to work on for at least several lifetimes. If we move forward with these challenges for self, we can avoid becoming overfocused on and reactive to that other party.

So, Who's Responsible for Claire's Depression?

When something goes wrong in a family, we naturally look for someone to blame. Or perhaps we point the finger at two or three people. But Claire's depression, like any serious problem, was probably several hundred years in the making; it may have been affected by issues, patterns, and events that were passed down over many generations. Whatever our particular theory (and there are countless biological and psychological theories that will continue to change and be enlarged over time), we are best to be humble. There is far more that we *don't* know about human behavior than we *do* know. Our most esteemed experts would have, at best, only a partial and incomplete explanation of Claire's depression.

So, who is responsible for curing Claire's depression or solving her problem? There is only one person who can do this job, although others will try, and that is Claire. It is *her* job to use her competence to become the best expert on her self and to figure out how she will work on her problem. Others may make it easier or harder for her to work toward recovery, but the challenge is hers.

But what of all the good work Linda did? Didn't this help Claire? Linda got out of the middle of the relationship between Claire and their mother. She modified her overfunctioning. She opened up communication. She set limits with Claire and defined a position around the suicide issue while letting Claire know she cared about her. She shared her underfunctioning side. She worked to deintensify her focus on Claire and to put more energy into her own issues, such as her distance from her father. She stayed in touch. These are extremely helpful actions that we as family members can take when someone we care about is underfunctioning. However, that's all they are. Only helpful. They do not solve the other person's problem, nor is doing so our job.

To what end, then, did Linda change? The work she did will give her the best chance of keeping her own anxiety down, having solid family relationships, and proceeding with her own life as well as possible. Linda's changed behavior will also make it easier, rather than harder, for Claire to use her competence to work on her own problem. But there is nothing that Linda or her parents can do to either cause or cure Claire's depression. Claire will either find a way to work on her problem when she is ready—or she will not.

12

Our Mother/
Her Mother/Our Self

Before all else, we are daughters. Our relationship with our mother is one of the most influential in our lives and it is never simple. Even when we have been separated from our mother at birth—or later by death or circumstance—a deep and inexplicable bond connects daughter to mother, mother to daughter.

As adult daughters, this bond may be one of profound ambivalence. We may still be blaming our mother, trying to change or fix her, or we may still be keeping our emotional distance. We may be absolutely convinced that our mother is "impossible," that we have tried everything to improve things and that nothing works.

So, what is the problem?

The problem is that these are cardinal signs of being stuck in this key relationship. They are signs we have not negotiated our ultimate separateness from our mother, nor have we come to terms with her separateness from us. If we are still blaming our mother, we cannot truly accept our self. If we are still fighting or distancing, we are *reacting* to the intensity in this relationship rather than working on it. And if we fail to carve out a clear and authentic self in this arena, we won't have a clear and separate self to bring to other important relationships. As we have seen, whatever goes unresolved and unaddressed in our first family will go underground—and then pop up somewhere else, leaving us in a more shaky, vulnerable position with others.

By working on the task of reconnecting with our mother, we can bring to this relationship a greater degree of self and can learn to appreciate the "separate self" of this woman we call mother. We hear much about how a *mother* impedes her daughter's separateness and independence. We hear less about the *daughter's* own difficulty in experiencing her mother as a separate and different "other," with a personal history of her own.

In the pages that follow, we examine the changes that one woman, Cathy, was able to make in her relationship with her mother. Her story, like others I have shared, will illustrate the process of moving toward a more mature intimacy in which we can define the self and respect the emotional separateness of the other. While we have already examined this process in depth, Cathy's struggle will allow us to summarize and appreciate anew the complexity of change and help us to think further about our own relationships.

Cathy and Her Mom

"My mother is really impossible!" concluded Cathy after a recent evening in her parent's home. "She's totally defensive and she won't listen to anything I say!"

"What was it you were wanting her to hear?" I inquired. Cathy had been in psychotherapy only briefly, and I knew relatively little about her family.

"First of all, there are a whole bunch of things I've been angry about for a long time, and I wanted to clear the air. I figured it would be good to get things out in the open, instead of just sitting on my feelings."

Cathy paused to catch her breath and then continued, with obvious exasperation in her voice, "My mother simply cannot deal with my anger! Each time I'd raise a legitimate complaint, she would say, 'Yes, but . . .' and then she'd end up criticizing *me*. I tried to get through to her—but as always, it's impossible."

"What were you trying to get across to her?" Cathy still hadn't answered my earlier question.

"First of all, my younger brother, Dennis, is doing poorly in school, and my mother constantly grills him about whether he's trying drugs and why he's out till midnight with his friends. That's one thing I was trying to give her feedback about. Then, there's the way she treats my dad, making all sorts of decisions for him. And finally, she's always intruding into my life, especially since my divorce. She worries constantly about my son, Jason, and she is always telling me to pray to Jesus. She needs to be totally in control of everything and everybody, and the whole family is suffering."

"Anything else?" I asked, as if that wasn't enough.

"Well, those were my main agenda items for this visit. But of course there's more. A lifetime more."

Cathy's complaints sounded familiar. I had heard them countless times before—in countless forms—from countless women in psychotherapy. And Cathy, like Linda and like so many of us, was doing the very things with her mom that only served to preserve the status quo. She blamed her mother for unilaterally "causing" family problems. She assumed that she (Cathy) was the expert on how her mother should handle her relationships (such as with Cathy's dad and brother). And she alternated between silence and distance, on the one hand, and fighting and blaming, on the other. As we have seen, these behaviors keep us stuck by ensuring that problems will not be addressed in a productive way, that old patterns will not be changed, and that intimacy will not occur.

Mother-Blame/Mother-Guilt

Cathy, like the rest of us, approached her mother, Anne, with only the best intentions. Her intention was not to blame Anne and certainly not to hurt her. According to Cathy, she confronted her mother because she wanted to lay the groundwork for a better relationship and because she wanted to help Anne deal with other family problems.

"How do you understand the fact that your mother couldn't hear a word you said?" I knew the question was premature, because Cathy's reactivity to her mom was still so intense I could not expect her to reflect on this problematic relationship and, in particular, her part in maintaining it.

"Because she's so defensive. She just feels accused and tries to protect herself."

Without knowing Cathy's mother, I could safely assume Cathy was on target here. Anne felt accused and tried to protect herself; she became defensive. So, what else is new? Or, to put it differently, why shouldn't she?

Our mothers have let us all down because they have lived with impossible and crippling expectations about their role. It is natural for a mother to react to her daughter's criticisms with anxiety and guilt. In fact, guilt is woven into the very fabric of womanhood. As one family therapist puts it, "Show me a woman who doesn't feel guilt, and I'll show you a man." Feelings of guilt run deepest and are most ingrained in mothers, who are the first to be blamed and the first to blame themselves. For example, recall Adrienne's mother, Elaine (Chapter 5), who felt responsible both for having a retarded son and for not keeping him at home. Or Kimberly's mother (Chapter 9), who stayed awake at night thinking she had "caused" her daughter's lesbianism—or that others would see it that way.

Mother-guilt is not simply the personal problem of individual women. Rather, it stems naturally from a society which assigns mothers the primary responsibility for all family problems, excuses men from real fathering, and provides remarkably little support for the actual needs of children and families. A mother is encouraged to believe she *is* her child's environment, and that if only she is a "good enough" mother, her children will flourish. It is only natural that Cathy's mother was sensitive to blame, and defensive in response to being accused of not being a good enough mother. Only a remarkably flexible and secure mother would react otherwise.

Let's look more closely at how Cathy navigated her relationship with Anne, with an eye toward consolidating some of the lessons we have learned about changing our own part in the relationship dances that block intimacy and keep us stuck. Underlying most mother-daughter distance and conflict is anxiety about navigating separateness and independence in this key relationship—and the usual confusion about what "separateness" and "independence" really mean. Cathy thought confronting her mother was a courageous expression of her "real" and independent self. In fact, her behavior made it more difficult to achieve this goal.

A Matter of Differences

Cathy's relationship with Anne had always been strained, but it had gone from bad to worse following Cathy's divorce two years earlier. "Mother always made my business her business," explained Cathy, "but since I've been living alone with my son, Jason, she really tries to run my life."

According to Cathy, Anne expressed a never-ending concern about Jason's well-being and about Cathy's lack of religious values. "My mother worries that Jason has been traumatized by the divorce," Cathy said, "and she doesn't like the way I'm raising him. Religion is the biggest issue between us. Saturday I had Mother over for lunch and I had to sit through her religion lecture for the tenth time—and in front of Jason!"

Anne's "religion lecture" took a variety of forms, but it basically boiled down to the following: First, Anne believed that Cathy should take Jason to church on Sundays. Second, Anne wanted Cathy to give religion a more central place in her own life. Whenever Cathy expressed sadness or anger over the divorce, Anne instructed her to pray. Cathy had no patience with her mother's advice or criticism (although Cathy had plenty of advice and criticism for Anne), and she did not like her parenting to be criticized in front of her son.

Cathy felt chronically tense in her mother's presence. She believed she had tried everything she could to change their antagonistic relationship; when nothing changed, she diagnosed the situation as hopeless. In reality, however, Cathy had explored no option other than moving from silence and distance to fighting and blaming, and back again. And both she and her mother acted as if they were the best expert on the other.

The Old Dance

Although Cathy periodically confronted Anne about her mismanagement of *other* family relationships, Cathy more typically said nothing at all when *she* was the target of her mother's criticism and unsolicited advice. She excused her failure to speak out. "My mother won't listen; it only makes things worse. My mother just can't hear the truth!" Sometimes Cathy refused to see Anne: "Mother upset me so much after the divorce that I avoided her for several months. If I could have afforded the plane ticket, I would have gone to China."

By distancing and failing to speak out on her own behalf, Cathy kept her relationship with her mother calm. As a way of managing anxiety, distancing *does* work in the short run, and that's why we do it. However, in Cathy's attempts to preserve a pseudoharmonious "we," Cathy was sacrificing the "I." *The degree to which we can be clear with our first family about who we are, what we believe, and where we stand on important issues will strongly influence the level of "independence" or emotional maturity that we bring to other relationships.* If Cathy continues to avoid taking a stand on emotionally important issues, she will remain "stuck together" with her mom, and she will be on less solid ground in other relationships as well.

According to Cathy, she did occasionally "take a firm stand" and "share her true feelings." But just what did she mean by this? Typically, it meant that Cathy moved from silently seething in her mother's presence to letting it all hang out. Like a pendulum that has swung too far in one direction, she occasionally went to the other extreme with

Anne. When this happened, Cathy would come to therapy describing an interaction that sounded like a confrontation between Godzilla and *Tyrannosaurus rex.* "My mother went off on her religion kick again, and I told her that she just used religion as a crutch—a simple solution to all of life's problems. Things escalated and she ended up storming out of the house in her usual dramatic fashion."

Fighting and blaming, like silence and distance, protected both mother and daughter from successfully navigating their separateness from each other. Again, "separateness" does not mean emotional distance, which is simply one means of managing anxiety or emotional intensity. *Rather, separateness refers to the preservation of the "I" within the "we" —the ability to acknowledge and respect differences and to achieve authenticity within the context of connectedness.* How well we do this within our own kinship group largely determines our capacity for intimacy elsewhere, and influences how well we will manage other relationships throughout our lives.

Defining a Self

One of the first steps in achieving independence or in "defining a self" is to move beyond silence and fighting, to begin making clear statements about our own beliefs and our position on important issues. For example, Cathy might choose a time when things were relatively calm to say to Anne, "Mom, I would really prefer that you don't discuss how I'm bringing up Jason in front of him. If you'd like to talk about my not taking him to church, let's find a time when just the two of us can discuss it."

Cathy can learn to address the real issues at hand rather than marching off to battle without knowing what the war is really about. In the old pattern, Cathy argued endlessly with her mother about whether Jason needed to go to church, and about the role of religion in their family life. Such fights were bound to go nowhere, and they kept Cathy stuck for two reasons: First, Cathy was trying to change her mother's mind, which was not possible. Second, she was behaving as if there were only one truth (about religion, child-rearing, or anything else), which both she and Anne should agree on.

The fact is that Cathy and Anne are two separate people who understandably have two different views of the world. Failure to appreciate this blocks real intimacy, which requires a profound respect for differences. We have seen how vulnerable we all are to confusing closeness with sameness and behaving as if we should share a common brain or heart with the other person.

This is especially true between mothers and daughters. With our beliefs about "women's place" shifting so dramatically over the past two decades, it is no surprise that mothers, in particular, may react strongly to their daughters' declaration of themselves as *different* from the generations of women who have come before. A mother may unconsciously experience such difference as disloyal or as a betrayal—a negative comment on her own life, or perhaps simply a reminder of options and choices that were unavailable to her. And of course, a daughter's "declaration of independence" can be especially hard for a mother who may feel she has nothing—not even a self—to return to after her children are grown. When women are taught that mothering is a "career" rather than a relationship, "retirement" becomes an understandable crisis. And because many daughters *do* handle their struggles with independence by distancing, blaming, or cutting off, then a mother's feeling of loss is understandably great. Mental health professionals may also contribute to the problem by instructing mothers "to separate" from their daughters, as if "to separate" means only giving something up, rather than working slowly toward a new and potentially richer kind of connectedness.

In sum, Cathy's job is to address the real issue in her relationship with Anne—the fact that she is a separate person with thoughts, beliefs, priorities, and values that differ from her mother's. To do this, Cathy must stop trying to change, criticize, or convince her mother; she must instead begin to share more about her own self, while respecting her mother's right to think, feel, and react differently.

For example, Cathy might say to Anne, "Mom, I know that religion has an important place in your life, but it's not where I'm at right now." If her mother begins to argue the point or criticize, Cathy can avoid getting drawn back into the old fight, because she knows from experience that intellectual arguments go nowhere and only keep her stuck. Instead, she might listen respectfully to everything Anne says and then merely reply, "Mom, I know how helpful your faith has been to you. But it's not my way." If Anne becomes hysterical and tells Cathy she is bringing disgrace to the family and causing her mother to have a coronary, Cathy can say, "I'm sorry if I'm hurting you, Mom, because that's not my intention." When her mother brings up religion for the 120th time, Cathy can joke with her or lightly reply, "I understand your feelings, but I see things differently."

Sound simple? Such conversations require a lion's share of courage, because they bring the separateness between mother and daughter into bold relief and, as a result, evoke tremendous anxiety. If Cathy stays on track, her mother will react strongly to her daughter's changed behavior by upping the ante in some way, perhaps by criticizing and blaming Cathy, or by threatening to sever their relationship.

It is important to keep in mind that countermoves or "Change back!" reactions occur whenever we move toward a higher level of assertiveness, separateness, and maturity in a key relationship. When we are the one initiating a change, we easily forget that countermoves express anxiety, not lack of love, and they are always predictable. The challenge for Cathy is to hold on to a process view of change, and to sit still through her mother's countermoves without returning more than temporarily to the old pattern of distancing or fighting. She can learn to sound like a broken record, if necessary, in the face of countless "tests." We have seen how change in a stuck relationship often feels like an uphill battle. It can require stamina and motivation, as well as a good sense of humor, to keep moving against the enormous and inevitable resistance from both within and without.

Moving Toward the Hot Issues

How did Cathy actually do in this difficult task of "defining a self" with her mother? In some areas, quite well. For example, she was extremely clear and consistent with Anne about *not* discussing her parenting in front of Jason, and when her mother continued to "drop comments" in front of him, Cathy didn't take the bait. Instead, she'd joke with her mother or otherwise deflect her criticisms—and then bring up the subject later when Jason was not within hearing distance. Cathy did not get intense or reactive to her mother's "tests" and countermoves, and she was clear in her own mind that *she* would not participate in arguments about Jason in his presence—even when "invited" to do so.

Whenever the religion issue came up, however, Cathy had a far more difficult time. As she put it, "Every time my mother brings Jesus into the conversation or tells me to pray, I just clutch and lose it." Over time, Cathy gained more control over her behavior, but not over her strong emotional response. "When my mother gets going about religion, I get knots in my stomach and I just feel like screaming at her," explained Cathy. "The best I can do is to drop the issue and change the subject."

In one sense, Cathy is correct. The worst time to try to discuss a hot issue in a stuck relationship is when we are feeling angry or tense. Emotional intensity only makes people more likely to *react* to each other in an escalating fashion rather than to think objectively and clearly about their dilemma. If Cathy is clutching inside and feels like screaming, it's not a bad idea for her to drop the issue, change the subject, take a walk, or escape to the bathroom to seek temporary distance. Over the long haul, however, Cathy will do best if she can begin to move *toward* the subject of religion, to get a broader perspective on her mother's attitude and on her own strong emotional response to the subject. How can Cathy move toward opening up such a difficult subject?

The Broader Picture

Every family has its hot issues, which come down the pike, unprocessed in one generation and played out in the next. In Cathy's family, religion was one hot issue, especially between mother and daughter. You can recognize a hot issue in your family if a subject is focused on incessantly and intensely, or if it cannot be talked about at all. You can be sure it's a hot issue if you clutch inside when the subject comes up.

How could Cathy gain a calmer and more objective perspective on this hot issue in her family? First, she had to widen the focus a bit. To this end, I asked Cathy a number of questions to help her think about what religion meant to her family in previous generations. What was the place of religion in her mother's own family as she was growing up? Did her mother have differences of opinion with her own mother; if so, were they openly expressed? If such differences existed, how were they handled? How would her grandmother have reacted if Anne had became a self-declared atheist, like Cathy? How did Cathy's mother arrive at her religious and spiritual beliefs, and in what way did they evolve over time? At what age did her mother become religious, and what significantly influenced her religiosity? Who else in the previous generations had "left" religion? Who had been most involved in it? What else was going on when important changes in such involvements occurred?

It was understandably difficult for Cathy to approach her mother calmly, factually, and warmly about this particular subject. By definition, the hot issues in a family can't easily be discussed objectively and productively, and of course, the more we avoid discussion, the hotter they become. When Cathy was finally able to get the subject out on the table, in a genuinely curious and uncritical way, the deep emotionality surrounding the subject of religion in her family took on a new meaning for her.

A Piece of History

What ultimately emerged in Cathy's talks with her mother was the story of a traumatic, early loss in her mother's own family. When Anne was five years old, her three-year-old brother, Jeff, died after ingesting a toxic substance in the family home. In addition to profound feelings of loss, Cathy's grandmother must have struggled with a deep sense of guilt and despair regarding her own fantasied or real contribution to Jeff's death. She was the only person home with her son when the tragic event occurred.

Anne didn't know all the facts surrounding her brother's poisoning, because this loss became the hot issue in her own family—a taboo subject that was never discussed. From what Anne was able to share with Cathy, it seemed that her mother's own religious attitudes had intensified after Jeff's death, as she struggled to survive the loss. On those rare occasions when Jeff's name was mentioned, it was only in the most *positive* of religious terms: "God takes only the best for himself." "It was God's will." "Jeff is happy with God." "God wanted Jeff with him." Both parents clung desperately to this one framing of the tragedy, in a manner that discouraged other questions and reactions from emerging openly among family members.

Cathy had long known that her mother had lost a brother in childhood. But this fact had not been *real* to Cathy, nor had she thought about its actual impact on her mother's life. Now Cathy learned that Anne had never seen her way clear to question her *own* mother's religious beliefs —in fact, after the tragedy, Anne "protected" her mother by suppressing differences of opinion on many issues. Anne believed that religion was her mother's lifeline, that it quite literally kept her mother alive. To question her mother's assumptions, or even to believe differently herself, was not an option for Anne. And now her own daughter, Cathy, was disavowing *all* religion, which only reactivated the old buried feelings surrounding a tragic death that had never been processed and emotionally put to rest.

This new information allowed Cathy to make connections between two generations of mothers and daughters. Anne's "solution" to the difficult challenge of selfhood with her own mother was to inhibit and deny expressions of difference, not only in religious matters, but also concerning any number of important issues. Cathy's "solution" was the opposite—which was really the same. Cathy was trying to define a separate self by being as *unlike* her mother as possible. If Anne said "apples," Cathy was sure to say "bananas." *Having to be different from our mother expresses our real self no more than having to be the same.*

The Pluses for Cathy

How did it affect Cathy to learn more about this crucial event in her mother's own family? For one thing, Cathy was able to feel somewhat more empathic and less reactive when the subject of religion reared its controversial head. In fact, reflecting on the impact of Jeff's death allowed Cathy to put many of her mother's "obnoxious behaviors" in a broader perspective. For example, Cathy felt extremely bugged by her mother's anxiety about her brother and especially about Jason's well-being after his parents' divorce. Cathy was now able to see how her mother's anxiety in these relationships was fueled by the intense, unresolved mourning process in her own family. Surely the issue of the survival and well-being of sons was an understandably loaded one for Anne.

As Cathy began to detoxify the hot issue of religion by getting it out on the table and broadening her perspective, she was also able to think through her own beliefs on this subject more clearly. Cathy's position on religion ("I'd drop dead before I'd bring Jason into a church") was a reactive one, and no more a statement of independent values than was her mother's desperate clinging to religious clichés. As Cathy began to view the legacy of religious values in her family through a wide-angle lens, thus gaining a better sense of her mother's own history, she was able to better formulate her *own* views on religion without mindlessly rebelling against the beliefs of two generations of women before her.

Perhaps most important of all, Cathy's conversations with her mother allowed her to experience Anne as a "real person," a separate and different "other" who had a personal history of her own. *Gathering information about our parents' lives, whether they are living or dead, is an important part of gaining a clear self, rooted in a factual history of our family's development.* And as Cathy discovered, information about each previous generation alters and enlarges the very meaning of behavior. For example, as Cathy learned more about her maternal grandparents' traumatic immigration from Poland, including the massive losses and severed ties that each experienced at the time, she viewed their "extreme" personalities in a new light. Her earlier glib and critical response ("Those folks became religious fanatics after the kid died") was replaced by a respectful appreciation of her grandparents' multiple losses and their strength and courage in finding a way to continue their lives after losing their son.

A Postscript: So You Think You Know Your Family?

Like many of us, Cathy began therapy convinced that she knew her family. This meant that she had stories to tell about family members and a psychiatric diagnosis for just about everyone on her family tree. But the stories we tell about our family frequently reflect the polarities that characterize systems under stress ("My mother the Saint," "Uncle Joe the Sinner") and have little to do with the complexity of real people and actual history. When anxiety has been high, we know who the good guys are, we know who the bad guys are, and we know whose camp we are in.

If we can move toward gathering a more factual history of our family, and enlarge the context over several generations, we will gain a more objective perspective on family members. We can begin to see our parents, as well as other relatives, as *real people in context* who have both strengths and vulnerabilities—as all human beings do. And if we can learn to be more objective in our own family, other relationships will be a piece of cake.

The best way to begin this process is to work on your own genogram, or family diagram. Instructions on doing a genogram can be found in the appendix at the back of this book. On the face of it, this may seem like a simple and straightforward task, as a genogram is nothing more than a pictorial representation of family facts. The facts included on a genogram are dates of births, deaths, marriages, separations, divorces, and major illnesses, as well as the highest level of education and occupation for each family member.

If you approach the task seriously, you will find that your genogram is a springboard to thoughts about many of the ideas presented in this book—or you may simply notice things of interest. You may find, for example, that you have considerable information about one side of your family and almost none about the other. You may become clearer about the hot issues and cutoffs on your family tree as you are confronted with the facts that you *don't* have and that you are uncomfortable asking about. ("How and when did Aunt Jess die?" "What is the exact date of my adoption?") You may begin to notice certain patterned ways that anxiety is managed on a particular side of the family; for example, on your father's side there may be considerable distance, including a good number of divorces, cutoffs, and people who don't speak to each other. You may observe there are few people on your family tree that you have a real relationship with— and that those relationships you *do* have are pretty intense.

The genogram is also your source of important anniversary dates and provides a context for understanding why relationships intensified or fell apart at a particular time. The ages of those who suffered losses, deaths, divorces, or downhill slides in the previous generations will give clues as to what years (as well as what issues) were particularly anxious ones in your past, and what ages may be particularly loaded ones for you in the future. You may notice certain patterns and core triangles repeating over generations or you may make observations about sibling position, as when Adrienne (Chapter 5) identified an issue around second-born sons in her family. The more facts you gather, the more questions you will generate.

Over time, working on a genogram helps us to pay primary attention to the self in our most important and influential context—our first family. It helps us to view relationship problems from a much broader perspective, over generations, rather than focusing narrowly on a few family members who may be idealized or blamed. As we are able to think more objectively about our family legacy and connect with more people on our family tree, we become clearer about the self and better able to take a position in our family, as Cathy did with Anne. It is not that we can ever gather a complete family history or be entirely objective about our own family. Obviously we can't. But we can work on it.

13

Reviewing Self-Focus: The Foundations of Intimacy

Compared to the Good Old Days (or the Bad Old Days, depending on how you look at it), prescriptions for intimacy are improving. We are now encouraged, at least in principle, to bring to our relationships nothing less than a strong, assertive, separate, independent, and authentic self. Yet these agreeable adjectives have become cultural clichés, their meanings trivialized or obscured. Popular notions of "selfhood" do not easily translate into clear guidelines for genuine intimacy and solid connectedness with others. In the name of either *protecting* or *asserting* the self, we may fail to take a position on something that matters or we may cut off from significant others, operate at their expense, or behave as if we have the truth of the universe.

I hope that this book has helped you appreciate the challenge of intimacy and all that it requires. Working toward intimacy is nothing short of a lifelong task. The goal is to be in relationships where the separate "I-ness" of both parties can be appreciated and enhanced, and where neither competence nor vulnerability is lost sight of in the self or the other. Intimacy requires a clear self, relentless self-focus, open communication, and a profound respect for differences. It requires the capacity to stay emotionally connected to significant others during anxious times, while taking a clear position for self, based on one's values, beliefs, and principles.

Laying the groundwork for intimacy is such a difficult challenge because what we do "naturally" will naturally take us in the wrong direction. As we have seen, our normal and reflexive ways of managing anxiety inevitably lead us to participate in patterns, polarities, and triangles that keep us painfully stuck. The higher and more chronic the anxiety, the more entrenched the pattern—and the more courage and motivation we must summon to sustain even a small change.

How You Can Best Use This Book

Go slowly and thoughtfully, for starters. The book's lessons are far too complex to translate into a list of how-to skills, although careful attention to each woman's story will provide you with more than enough ideas about what you might work on for the next decade. My first book, *The Dance of Anger,* lays out clear and specific guidelines for changing stuck relationship patterns. If you are interested in learning more about triangles, reactivity, styles of managing anxiety (pursuing, distancing, overfunctioning, underfunctioning, and child-focus), and countermoves, I suggest that you read *The Dance of Anger* as well. Each book will help you appreciate and consolidate the lessons of the other. You may also decide to start a *"Dance"* group with other women, using these books as a springboard for discussion and for work on important relationships.

You will make the best use of this book if you are willing to struggle with *theory* rather than to focus narrowly on *tech-*

nique. When a relationship is going badly, or not going at all, we obviously want "techniques"—that is, we want to know what we can *do* to make things different. We may want a six-step program to fix things, a list of Do's and Don'ts, and (if we're honest) new maneuvers to change or shape up the other person. Even the best how-to advice, however, will at best yield short-lived results unless we struggle to understand the underlying theory or principles—in this case, a theory about how anxiety is managed and how relationship systems operate under stress.

The fact is, there are no techniques to "make intimacy happen," although countless self-help books offer this promise. Intimacy can happen only after we work toward a more solid self, based on a clear understanding of our part in the relationship patterns that keep us stuck.

The principles in this book may sound clear and simple when they are illustrated through the lives of other women. But when you try to apply what you have learned to your own relationships, you will see how quickly complexities and ambiguities arise. In this final chapter, I will help you to review and consolidate some important concepts that provide a foundation for thinking about intimacy. The more solid your understanding, the more clearly you will make your own decisions about how, when, if, and with whom you want to experiment with change. Let's look first at *feelings and reactivity,* and then at the complex principle of *self-focus.*

Thinking About Feelings

When I started writing this book, I asked eight people to define "an intimate relationship." The majority responded with a variation of the same theme: "A relationship where you can express your true feelings." The word "feelings" was unanimously emphasized, their free and spontaneous expression highlighted. I would agree: A truly intimate relationship is one in which we can be who we are, which means being open about our selves. Obviously the sharing of feelings is an integral part of intimacy.

And yet if you go back through this book, you will notice little focus on "getting out feelings" and none on "letting it all hang out." Rather, I have emphasized observing, thinking, planning, and learning to stay calm in the midst of intensity. Does this mean that feelings are wrong or bad, or that their full and spontaneous expression will always impede rather than facilitate the process of intimacy and change?

Certainly not. In flexible relationships, the emotional tone we use to take a position becomes relatively unimportant—a matter of personal style. With my husband, children, and certain friends, for example, I occasionally engage in impassioned arguments about "who's right," and if things don't get too stuck, I enjoy these exchanges. At certain times, however, and in other relationships, I will proceed with as much thoughtfulness and calm as I can muster.

It is always important for us to be *aware* of feelings. Our feelings exist for good reason and so deserve our attention and respect. Even uncomfortable feelings that we might prefer to avoid, such as anger and depression, may serve to preserve the dignity and integrity of the self. They signal a problem, remind us that business cannot continue as usual, and ultimately speak to the necessity for change. But as I explained in *The Dance of Anger, venting* feelings does not necessarily *solve* the problem causing us pain.

Venting our feelings may clear (or muddy) the air, and may leave us feeling better (or worse). When we live in close quarters with someone, strong emotional exchanges are just a predictable part of the picture and it's nice to know that our relationships can survive or even be enhanced by them. But venting feelings, *in and of itself,* will not change the relationship dances that block real intimacy and get us into trouble. In stuck relationships, venting feelings may only rigidify old patterns, ensuring that change will not occur.

In some instances, a passionate display of intensity is a turning point, even in a stuck relationship, because it indicates to ourselves and others that we "really mean it." It is part of a process in which we move toward clarifying the limits of what is acceptable and what is not. But just as frequently the opposite is true: reactivity serves to "let off steam," following which things will continue as usual. Reactivity and intensity often breed more of the same. When it becomes chronic, reactivity blocks *self-focus,* which is the only foundation on which an intimate relationship can be built.

Emotions are not bad or wrong, and women certainly are not "too emotional," as we have often been told. The ability to recognize and express feelings is a strength, not a weakness. It does not help anyone, however, to be buffeted about by feelings or to drown in them. It *does* help to be able to think about our feelings. By "thinking," I do *not* mean intellectualizing or distancing from emotional issues, which men tend to do especially well. I simply mean that we can reflect on our feelings and make conscious decisions about how, when, and with whom we want to express them.

Even as we strive for objectivity, it is not easy to distinguish between true emotionality and anxiety-driven reactivity.

When Adrienne (Chapter 5) cried with her dad about his impending death, they were sharing an emotional experience. But when she avoided dealing with his cancer—and instead fought with or distanced from her husband—that was reactivity. When Linda told her sister, Claire, how terrified she was of losing her, and later shared how scared she was that they would end up as distant as their mother and their aunt Sue, she was in touch with her real feelings. But when she angrily lectured her sister or mother about what they should do differently, that was reactivity. Reactivity is an anxiety-driven response that blocks a truly intimate exchange—one that encourages the open sharing of thoughts and feelings, as well as problem solving around difficult issues.

Because anxiety will always be hitting us from all quarters, reactivity is simply a fact of emotional life. As we have seen, the question is reactivity . . . and then what? To move toward a more gratifying togetherness and authentic emotional exchange, we may first need to deintensify the situation to lower the anxiety. When an important relationship is stuck, we become powerful and courageous agents of change by making a new move in a low-key way, by taking a new position with humor and a bit of teasing, by making our point in a paragraph or two rather than in a long treatise. Trying out new steps slowly and calmly is also what allows us to keep in check our own anxiety and guilt about change, so that we can stay on course and stay *self-focused* when the powerful countermoves start rolling in.

Understanding Self-Focus

When couples enter therapy for "intimacy problems," they are invariably other-focused; that is, they see the other person as the problem and they believe the solution is for that person to change. I use the term "couple" here in the broadest sense, to mean any and all ongoing relationships between two persons.

What happens if a couple remains other-focused over time? *She* continues to insist that the only way the relationship will improve is for him to become more responsible. *He* says that instead she must become less critical and more sensitive to his needs. *What happens is that no change will occur.* I have yet to see a relationship improve unless at least one individual can give up their negative or worried focus on the other and put that same energy back into his or her own life.

Every courageous act of change that I've described in this book, like those in our own lives, requires a move toward greater selfhood or self-focus. Whether the other party is our lover, spouse, child, sibling, parent, friend, or boss, self-focus requires us to give up our nonproductive efforts to change or fix the other party (which is not possible) and to put as much energy into working on the self. Only then can we move out of stuck patterns and create a new dance.

We need to understand, however, that self-focus does *not* mean self-blame. It does *not* mean that we view our selves as the "cause" of our problems, or that we view our struggles as being isolated from the broader context of family and culture. It certainly does not mean that we remain silent in the face of discrimination, unfairness, and injustice.

To clarify the point, let's momentarily consider the changes brought about by the second wave of feminism. None of these changes could have occurred had we denied and disqualified our anger at men or maintained a narrow focus on the question "What's wrong with me?" At the same time, however, feminists could not have become effective agents of change if we had gotten stuck in reactive gear and focused our primary energies on trying to transform men or make them into nicer and fairer people. The women's movement changed and challenged all our lives because feminists recognized that if we did not clarify our own needs, define the terms of our own lives, and take action on our own behalf, *no one else would do it for us*. Thus, feminists began busily writing women back into language and history, establishing countless programs and services central to women's lives, starting new scholarly journals and women's studies programs in universities, to name just a few actions. Only in response to our changing our own selves, and to our taking individual and collective action on our own behalf, would men be called on to change.

Moving toward self-focus does not mean narrowing our perspective. To the contrary, it means viewing our intimacy problems in the broadest possible context of family and culture. This broader perspective helps us think more calmly and objectively about our situation and how we might change our own part in it. Our part in it is the only thing we can change.

Self-Focus and Humility

Self-focus requires more than an appreciation of the fact that we cannot change the other person and that doing so is not our job. It also requires a transformation of consciousness, a different worldview than what comes naturally. I refer here to the challenge of truly appreciating how little we can know about human behavior and how impossible it is to be an expert on the other person. As I emphasized at the start of this book, we cannot know how and when another person is ready to work on something and how she or he (and others) will tolerate the consequences of change. These things are difficult enough to know for our own selves. Yet in the name of love and good intentions, we readily assume an "I-know-what's-best-for-you" attitude. This attitude precludes the possibility of intimacy and makes it much harder for other persons to assume responsibility for solving their own problems and managing their own pain.

Self-Focus and Being a Self

At the same time, we have seen that taking the focus off the other does not mean silence, distance, cutoff, or a policy of "anything goes." Rather, it means that *as we become less of an expert on the other, we become more of an expert on the self.* As we work toward greater self-focus, we become *better* able to give feedback, to share our perspective, to state clearly our values and beliefs and then stand firmly behind them. As Adrienne and Linda's stories have illustrated, we can do this as part of defining a self, and not because we have the answers for the other person. The following story shows another example of a woman working toward greater self-focus.

Regina's husband, Richard, became severely depressed after losing his job and his father in the same year. He spent more and more time in bed, isolating himself from others and failing to put much effort into seeking new employment. For several months, Regina, a natural overfunctioner, organized herself around his problem. She did double-duty housework and childcare, because Richard said he couldn't handle it. She circled help-wanted ads in the newspaper and brought Richard leads about job openings. She turned down social engagements he wished to avoid. Increasingly, she accommodated to her husband's problem or tried to solve it. Richard's depression persisted and worsened.

After several months, Regina was feeling exhausted and out of sorts. She told Richard that she wasn't taking good care of herself and that she needed to make doing so a priority. She joined an exercise class, began going out with friends, and accepted social invitations even though Richard stayed home. She also stopped covering up or functioning for him. For example, when the phone rang and he said, "Tell Al I'm out. I'm too depressed to talk," she handed him the phone and said warmly, "Tell him yourself." When Richard insisted that she keep his depression a secret, she clarified a position she could comfortably live with. "Look, I won't tell your mom or Al, because I figure that's your job. But I *have* talked with my parents and Sue about it, because I can't have a relationship with them and keep such a big secret." Increasingly, Regina struggled to clarify a responsible position for herself and she stopped organizing her behavior around Richard's symptoms and his demands.

When Richard continued to remain in hibernation, Regina walked into the bedroom one Saturday and said, "Richard, if this continues for one more week, *I'm* going to be so depressed myself that I'm going to crawl into that bed with you. Then this family will really be in a fix. So what are we going to do about it?"

These were *not just words* on Regina's part. She really meant it. She had no answers for him, although she had a few suggestions if he were interested. What she *did* know was that she could not continue with the status quo for much longer, for her own sake—and out of her concern for him and the family as well. At this point she was no longer willing to keep his depression a secret from any friends or family.

Regina ended up taking a bottom-line position that Richard had to do something because she could no longer live with the situation. Richard was briefly hospitalized and then began psychotherapy. Regina was able to give him lots of space to struggle with his depression because she empathized with his pain *without focusing on it.* She put her primary energy into her own problems, which she shared with him. And when he initially "couldn't listen," she addressed this with him over time ("Rich, I hear you saying that because your problems are so much more serious than mine, my feelings don't really count. The situation at work with Joe is real distressing to me and I need to be able to talk with you about it—if not now, then sometime soon").

This shift from other-focus to self-focus is particularly hard for overfunctioners who truly believe that the other person will die without our help. We may not pay attention to the fact that they may be dying *with* our help.

Does a shift toward self-focus bring intimacy into a troubled relationship? Not in the short run. When you set new limits and boundaries, the other may not respond positively. This is true whether you are telling your husband that you will no longer pack his lunch or informing your bulimic daughter that if she vomits in the morning, she has to clean up after herself, even if it makes her late for school. A move toward "more self" in a relationship is usually followed by anxiety (our own and the other person's) and countermoves ("How can you be so selfish?"). If we can hold to a new position, however, without distance or blame, intimacy may come later—or at least the relationship has the very best chance. *But you can't initiate a courageous act of change because the other person will love you for it.* The other person may not love you for it, at least not in the short run and possibly never.

Self-Focus and Emotional Separateness

As we become more self-focused, we define a responsible position in a relationship, based on our own values, beliefs, and principles rather than in reaction to how the other person chooses to define the relationship. As we have seen, this self-focus requires lowered reactivity and a high degree of emotional "separateness" from the other.

Consider Janine, a woman who married out of her own religion and converted to Catholicism. In response, her mother and an older brother would not attend the wedding and refused to acknowledge her as a family member. They did not respond to Janine's attempts to explain her decision to convert, nor to her pleas for greater flexibility and tolerance on their part. Their resolve to cut her off was so firm that neither acknowledged the arrival of a new granddaughter.

Janine was ultimately able to accept her mother and brother's decision, although she did not like it. As she gathered more information about her family history, she recognized that for several generations people in her family had cut off from each other around differences. There were two warring factions in her extended family, which included relatives who had not spoken to each other for many years. It was Janine's job to consider whether she wished to continue this pattern of managing anxiety and pass it down through the generations.

Janine ultimately decided that the position *she* would take in the family was one of connectedness rather than cutoff. Although her mother and brother had proclaimed her "dead," she sent each of them cards with brief notes on holidays, birthdays, and other life-cycle events. *In these communications, she did not attempt to change their minds or move them toward reconciliation.* She made clear to both her mother and brother that she understood the pain her conversion to Catholicism had brought them, and that she accepted the fact that they did not want to have a relationship with her. But she also explained that it was not possible for *her* to pretend she did not have a mother or brother. She simply found it too painful to deny the existence of people who were so important to her.

When Janine first decided that she would stay connected, she wrote her mother and brother a short note in which she mentioned her awareness of the many people in the family who did not speak to each other. She said that while she respected this as a necessary choice for some, she personally would feel devastated if she stopped speaking to a family member. Although Janine was clear about her own resolve to maintain some contact, she kept subsequent communications short and low-key, recognizing that to do otherwise would be to disregard the position of distance that her mother and brother had chosen to take. She also refrained from either criticizing or explaining them to other family members, thus avoiding triangles.

Four years later, Janine's mother called her. Earlier that week she had received a fiftieth birthday card that Janine had sent. She explained to Janine that she had been sitting in church that Sunday and suddenly realized that God did not want her to reject her daughter. "It is not God's will that I should lose a good daughter," she said with deep emotion. Then she pulled herself together and added matter-of-factly, "Life is too short for this. I want to see my grandchild." Janine's brother continued to avoid her at this time.

Would this reconciliation between Janine and her mother have taken place if Janine had responded to her mother's anger and cutoff with more anger and cutoff? We do not know. What was important was *Janine's* decision to take a position of responsible connectedness rather than cutoff, *whether or not her mother or brother ever spoke to her again.* Janine defined a position that allowed her to feel like a more solid and responsible individual in her own family. She initiated new steps in a family dance that had been ongoing for generations. This example, like many others we have seen, illustrates the "separateness" that self-focus requires. It is a separateness that ultimately allows for a more solid connectedness with others.

Thinking About Our First Family

Slowly moving toward *more connectedness* rather than *more distance* with members of our own kinship group is one of the best insurance policies for bringing a more solid self to other relationships. When we have few connections with extended family, and one or more cutoffs with a nuclear family member (a sibling or parent), our other relationships may resemble a pressure cooker, particularly if we start a family of our own. The degree to which we are distant and cut off from our first family is directly related to the amount of intensity and reactivity we bring to other relationships.

Of course the goal is not just to move toward connectedness—meaning *any* kind of connectedness. Rather, the challenge is to move toward a connectedness that preserves the dignity of the self and the other, allowing for the creation of real intimacy. Each example in this book illustrates a move in such a direction, and each woman's story is worth a careful rereading if you think it may apply to you.

Before you are inspired to plan your own courageous act of change, I suggest that you *first* do your own genogram (family diagram) and study it. This task may itself require courageous new behaviors, because you won't be able to get the necessary information without reconnecting with people on your own family tree (see appendix). As I mentioned at the conclusion of the previous chapter, paying attention to your genogram will help you stay self-focused, and you'll get a broader view of who is family, apart from the few people you interact with. Our current problems with intimacy are not "caused" by the bad things that one or two family members have done to us. They are part of a much larger, multigenerational picture of events, patterns, and triangles that have come down through many generations.

Your genogram can also help you evaluate the level of chronic anxiety in your family. How intense are the triangles? How pervasive is conflict and distance? Are there cutoffs among family members? How extreme are the overfunctioning-underfunctioning polarities?

To what extent have important issues in the family been processed and talked about? How open are the lines of communication? How much tolerance does your family have for differences? How easily do family members polarize around hot issues such as sex, religion, divorce, illness, responsibility to aging parents, and Uncle John's drinking? Extreme positions over the generations reflect chronically high anxiety, indicating that the process of change will require very slow and small moves on your part.

A Matter of Timing

Plodding slowly forward is probably a good idea for us all. If I keep repeating this point, it is because the examples in this book are bound to invite an overly ambitious attitude. I have described changes certain women have made over a period of years, sometimes with the help of therapy, and have condensed these changes into a chapter or even into a page or two. *This makes change look too easy, no matter what I say to the contrary.* Do remember that courageous acts of change include, and even require, small and manageable new moves, along with inevitable frustrations and derailments. How small (and how frustrating) depends on how hot the issue, how chronic the anxiety, and how entrenched the patterns. Trying to do too much will only give us a great excuse to end up doing nothing at all. Let's look at two brief illustrations of seemingly small moves, which required large amounts of courage.

A woman named Marsha worked in therapy for several years before she felt ready to ask her father the names and birthdates of her grandparents. Her father had been adopted at age four, after losing his mother in a flu epidemic. There were countless unanswered and unspoken questions. What happened to Marsha's grandfather after her grandmother died? Why didn't he—or some other family member—raise her father? What did her father know about his birth parents and their families? Marsha's father never spoke of his past and had become overinvolved in his wife's family. He also was vulnerable to severe depression—which Marsha was unconsciously attuned to—and the unspoken family rule was to never question Dad about his past or talk with him about anything emotionally important. On Marsha's genogram, her father's side was entirely bare in terms of biological kin.

Marsha herself was depressed and had sought therapy for this reason. She had no intimate relationships and not much sense of self. Her father was extremely intense and child-focused, reflecting the extreme degree of cutoff from his own family. *Asking her dad the names and birthdates of his birth parents was a courageous act of change that was all Marsha felt ready to do for quite some time.* It was, for Marsha, a significant first move toward selfhood and connectedness. She did it with her heart pounding in her chest, but she did it.

A year later (perhaps in response to changes that Marsha was making) her father began the equally courageous task of initiating a small move to track down his own roots. He had long stifled curiosity about his past out of loyalty to his adoptive parents and his profound inner trepidations about what he might discover. This prohibition under which he operated was an important factor in his depression and colored all his relationships. Although to this day he has chosen to learn "just a little bit," this little bit may make a significant difference in his life.

When patterns are entrenched and reactivity is high, it can be useful and sometimes necessary to enlist professional help. A friend of mine named Eleanor was in an extremely rigid triangle in which her parents were legally but not emotionally divorced and the intensity between them was so high that probably nothing short of her funeral would have gotten them in the same room together. Her part in the triangle was to be in her father's camp at the expense of a relationship with her mother, who had had multiple affairs during her marriage which she had lied about. Eleanor saw her father as the "done-in" spouse, and to wave his banner, she unconsciously sacrificed her relationship with her mother. This core triangle and Eleanor's inability to work on having a person-to-person relationship with each parent, *free from the intensity between them,* affected all of Eleanor's relationships. Eleanor's position in the triangle also made it *less likely* that her parents would tackle their unfinished marital business and really separate. Triangles, once they get "fixed," operate at everyone's expense.

Family systems therapists do not coach their clients to jump in and do something different. Eleanor met once a month with her therapist, working hard to become more objective about the emotional process in her own family. It took a long time before she could stop blaming her mother and view this core triangle in the context of other interlocking triangles and key family events that had occurred over several generations. Only *after* she had achieved this calmer, broader, and more objective perspective was she ready to think about slowly shifting her part in this core triangle.

Eleanor's first courageous act of change with her father was a low-key allusion to the fact that she had a mother. "I was mowing over at Mom's this morning and I think I got a bit too much sun," Eleanor said, moving on to talk about the unseasonably hot weather. If you are not impressed, that's because you don't know Eleanor and the family context.

A Postscript on Self-Focus: Having a Life Plan

In the dances we get stuck in, we can only change and control ourselves. Each person in a relationship, however, does not have equal power to make new moves. Children who are supported by their parents do not have the same power to create a new dance as do the adults. A woman who is one husband away from poverty does not have the same power as her spouse.

If we are truly convinced that we cannot live without our husband's support, our mother's inheritance, our current job, or the room in our parents' basement, our own bottom-line position may be "togetherness at any cost." We may not articulate this bottom line or even be conscious of it, but in such circumstances we may find it impossible to initiate and sustain courageous acts of change. Kimberly, for example, might not have felt free to share her lesbianism with her parents if they were paying her apartment rent and if she saw no other options for generating income.

Think of Jo-Anne, our anonymous letter-writer in Chapter 2 who, according to her own report, canceled her subscription to *Ms.* to save her marriage. She may engage in endless cycles of nonproductive fighting, complaining, and blaming. She may invite thousands of *Ms.* readers to join her camp, siding with her against her husband. But in the end, she *protects* rather than *protests* the status quo. Only *after* Jo-Anne is confident that she can ensure her safety, her survival, and some reasonable standard of living can she go to her husband and say, "I will not cancel my subscription to *Ms.* magazine." Only then can she maintain this position with dignity and firmness.

Paradoxically, we cannot navigate clearly within a relationship unless we can live without it. For women, this presents an obvious dilemma. Only a small minority of us have been encouraged to put our primary energy into *formulating a life plan that neither requires nor excludes marriage.* We may have generations of training to *not* think this way. Countless internal obstacles and external realities still block our path when it comes to planning for our own economic future and formulating long-range work and career goals. Yet such planning—which requires both personal and social change —not only ensures the well-being of the self but also puts us on more solid ground for negotiating relationships with intimate others.

My point here is not to undervalue the role of homemaker or of any unsalaried or underpaid worker. Women have been divided from each other by the media's invitation for "Moms" and "Career Women" to pit themselves against each other. The issue is not, nor has it ever been, whether homemaking is more or less valuable, challenging, or fulfilling than running a corporation, for who among us could begin to make such a judgment? The real issue is that the role of homemaker places many women in a position of profound economic vulnerability, particularly given the current divorce rate, the lack of high-level training and re-entry programs for displaced homemakers, the low or uncollectible child-care payments, and negligible alimony. These facts are reflected in the alarming statistics on the poverty of single mothers.

You may already be one of these statistics. Or you may unconsciously be so afraid of becoming a statistic that you are not yet ready to risk making a courageous act of change with someone you depend on.

Having a life plan means more than working to ensure economic security as best you can. It also means working toward clarifying your values, beliefs, and priorities, and then applying them to your daily actions. It means thinking about what talents and abilities you want to develop over the next two—or twenty—years. Obviously, a life plan is not static or written in stone, but is instead open to constant revision over time.

Finally, having a life plan does *not* mean adopting masculine values and pursuing career goals single-mindedly. Some of us may be striving to lighten our work commitments so we can spend more time with our friends and family, or in other pursuits such as spiritual development or the peace movement. What is significant about a life plan is that it can help us live our own lives (not someone else's) as well as possible. How we do this, and how we conduct our relationships with our own family of origin, is the most valuable legacy we can leave the next generation.

When we do *not* focus our primary energy on working on our own life plan, our intimate relationships suffer—just as they suffer when we cut off from our own kinship group to start a family of our own. Without a life plan, our intimate relationships carry too much weight. We begin to look to others to provide us with meaning or happiness, which is not their job. We want a partner who will provide self-esteem, which cannot be bestowed by another. We set up a situation in which we are bound to get overinvolved and overfocused on the other person's ups and downs because we are underfocused on the self.

Intimate relationships cannot substitute for a life plan. But to have any meaning or viability at all, a life plan must include intimate relationships.

How essential are intimate relationships, really? In my own life, there are times when I am either so anxious or so eager about personal projects that the most treasured people in my life feel like distractions; my highest priority is to be left alone to do what I want to do. At other times—such as when a real crisis hits my family—nothing is more important than the love of my family and my friends and the support of my community; so necessary is this love, and my connectedness to others, that nothing else seems to matter.

Obviously, we will have varying and changing needs for distance and connectedness throughout the life cycle, and even during the course of a week or a day. It is as normal to seek distance occasionally as it is to seek togetherness; there is no "right" amount of intimacy for all couples or for all relationships. But without a viable connectedness in our kinship group and community, we just won't do very well when the going gets tough. Since everyone's life includes some hardship and some tragedy, we can count on the going getting tough.

Throughout history, women have stood for connected-ness by working to maintain ties to past and future genera-tions. Unfortunately, we have often done this at the expense of the self, sacrificing personal and career goals central both to our self-esteem and to our economic security. Not sur-prisingly, men have had a complementary problem; they have tended to focus on moving up and measuring up, at the expense of responsible connectedness to past and future generations. The success, if not the survival, of our intimate relationships rests on our being able to get this in balance. So, too, does the success and survival of our world.

Epilogue

Just as the female legacy does not promote thinking in terms of a life plan, it is also not part of our legacy to view ourselves as powerful agents of change. Women often feel powerless to initiate change, whether in their personal lives or in the public sphere. Like our fairy tale heroines, we may believe that we have to lie helpless in the teeth of the wolf, or asleep in a glass coffin, until we can be rescued by a handsome prince. We have been told that our sex is passive-dependent —that it is men who take charge and make change happen in the real world.

Such feelings are understandable, because in reality, women have been deprived of power. Men chart the stars, create language and culture as we know it, record history as they see it, build and destroy the world around us, and continue to run every major institution that generates power, policy, and wealth. Men define the very "reality" that—until the current feminist movement—I, for one, accepted as a given. And although women throughout history have exercised a certain power as mothers, we have not created the conditions in which we mother, nor have we constructed the predominant myths and theories about "good mothering." Even today, there is no female equivalent of America's best-known child-rearing experts, Dr. Spock and Dr. Brazelton.

(This is not because women do not know as much about taking care of babies as men do.)

Because of our condition of inequality, it is easy to feel powerless and to view women as ineffective agents of change. But, as we are learning, nothing could be further from the truth. Over the past two decades, women and minorities have been excavating the rich treasure of their history. If you studied women's history today, you would be surprised and exhilarated by the lives of our foremothers—and stunned by how these women's pioneering accomplishments have been overlooked in our culture's great texts. A detailed genogram of your own family over three or four generations will likely help you discover the women on your own family tree who were bold and courageous pioneers of change. Knowing the strength of our own legacy is empowering.

This book has focused on individual change and intimacy, surely a personal subject. Yet it is my hope that we will work toward becoming more courageous and effective agents of social change as well. It is the larger context of our lives—which we call the "social," "political," "societal," or "cultural" context—that gives shape and form to our most intimate interactions and to our very definition of family.

Although the connections are not always obvious, personal change is inseparable from social and political change. Intimate relationships cannot flourish under conditions of inequality and unfairness. Indeed, all our intimate relationships will look entirely different to us in a future where women are truly valued and equally represented alongside men in every aspect of public life. Just *how* such relationships will look, and just *when* such a future will be, we can only begin to imagine—but we must continue to work for those relationships and that future.

— *Appendix: Creating a Genogram* —

A genogram, or family diagram, is a pictorial representation of the facts of a family system for at least three generations. It is a springboard to help you think about your family and a useful format for drawing a family tree.

The genogram is a widely used tool in psychotherapy and family assessment. Some therapists use it simply to keep track of the cast of characters and dates in a particular family. For others, the genogram serves as a rich source of hypotheses regarding complex family emotional patterns. The genogram shows the strengths and vulnerabilities of a particular individual, or a particularly troubled family relationship, in a much larger context to give new meanings to problems and behavior.

Although the genogram is widely used by therapists of varying orientations (as well as by family physicians, historians, biographers, and the like), it is most frequently associated with Bowen family systems theory. Additional sources of information about the genogram can be found at the end of this appendix.

Genogram Symbols

Because there is diversity in how genograms are drawn, other therapists may use symbols somewhat different from those shown here.

Female

Give name, age, birthdate (*b.*), highest level of education, occupation, significant health problems, and date of diagnosis (*dx*).

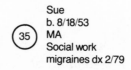

Sue
b. 8/18/53
MA
Social work
migraines dx 2/79

Male

Give name, age, birthdate, highest level of education, occupation, significant health problems, and date of diagnosis.

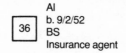

Al
b. 9/2/52
BS
Insurance agent

Index Person

You are the index person in your own genogram. Darken the outline of your gender symbol.

Death

Give age, date of death (*d.*), and cause.

b. 2/12/10
d. 3/21/80
Heart attack

b. 2/9/70
d. 5/12/75
Leukemia

Marriage

Give date of marriage (*m.*).
(Husband—left; wife—right)

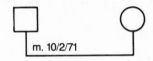

m. 10/2/71

Separation and Divorce

Separation (*s.*)—one diagonal line with date
Divorce (*d.*)—double diagonal line with date

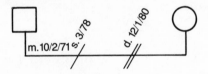

m. 10/2/71 s. 3/78 d. 12/1/80

Living Together or Significant Liaison

Draw a dotted line.

Multiple Marriages

(Mary was twice divorced before marrying Joe. Joe was widowed.)

Children

List in birth order beginning with oldest child on the left.

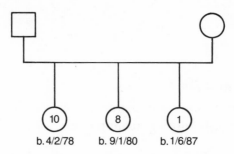

Twins

Indicate whether identical or fraternal (*I.* or *F.*).

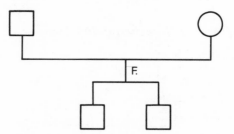

Adoption

Give birthdate, adoption date (*a.*), and any information about biological parents. (Do two genograms if information about birth family doesn't fit.)

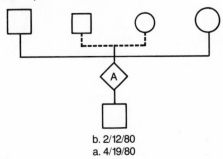

b. 2/12/80
a. 4/19/80

Foster Placement

Draw a dotted line from biological parents. Give date of foster placement (*F.P.*).

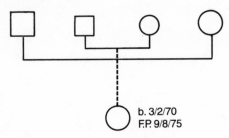

b. 3/2/70
F.P. 9/8/75

Pregnancy	*Miscarriage*	*Abortion*

3 mo.   9/1/72 or 9/1/72   3 mo.   3 mo.

Stillbirth or Intrauterine Death

4/12/81   2/18/72
7½ mo.

STRAUSS FAMILY GENOGRAM*

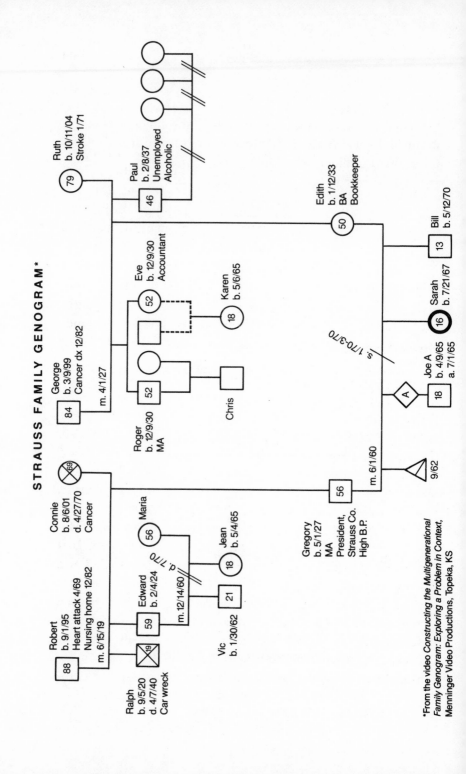

*From the video Constructing the Multigenerational
Family Genogram: Exploring a Problem in Context,
Menninger Video Productions, Topeka, KS

The Strauss Family Genogram

Sarah is the index person. She is the second child and first-born daughter in her sibling group. She has an older, adopted brother, Joe, whose entrance into the family followed a miscarriage. Sarah has a younger brother, Bill.

Sarah's father, Gregory, is the youngest of three sons. Gregory's older brother, Ralph, the first-born son, died in a car accident at the age of nineteen.

Sarah's mother, Edith, is a middle sibling. Her two older siblings, Roger and Eve, are twins. Eve had a child, Karen, with a man whom she chose not to marry. Edith's younger brother, Paul, has been married and divorced three times and has no children from his prior marriages. He is an alcoholic.

The genogram helps us to see that Sarah's father, Gregory, is at an important anniversary time. His youngest child, Bill, has turned 13, the age that Gregory was when Ralph was killed. Joe (who is in Ralph's sibling position) will soon be 19, the age when Ralph died. In addition, Sarah's three living grandparents are in very poor health. From this information alone one can speculate that this might be a stressful time in the life cycle of Sarah's family.

The genogram also suggests that Sarah's brother Bill was born into a particularly anxious emotional field. Just before Bill's birth his parents separated and reconciled and his paternal grandmother died of cancer. During the first year of Bill's life, his uncle Edward divorced and his maternal grandmother had a stroke. These events surrounding Bill's entrance into the family may have predisposed his early relationship with one or both parents to be emotionally intense. As a youngest child, Bill shares a common sibling position with his underfunctioning uncle Paul. How might this influence the relationship between Bill and his mother?

This genogram is only partially completed for purposes of illustration. Keep in mind that the usual amount of information included on a genogram are age, birthdate (and adoption date), highest level of education, occupation, significant health problems (including date of diagnosis), and date and cause of death for every circle and square on your family diagram and for as far back as you can search.

You may want to put other significant information on your genogram such as immigrations, retirements, and drug and alcohol problems, constructing your own shorthand or symbols to save space (for example, *ALC* or (A) for alcoholic). To keep your genogram from becoming too cluttered, use a large piece of oaktag or oversized paper and keep track of important information elsewhere (job changes, re-locations, ethnic and religious backgrounds, psychiatric hospitalizations, etc).

Bibliographical Information on Genograms*

Genograms in Family Assessment by Monica McGoldrick and Randy Gerson (New York: Norton, 1985). This informative book provides a detailed description of constructing a genogram along with an introduction to its underlying interpre-

---

* References on the theory and therapy of Dr. Murray Bowen, who pioneered the use of the genogram, can be found in the notes. While most sources are directed toward therapists, they are valuable reading for nonprofessionals as well.

tation and application. The authors use genograms of famous people such as Sigmund Freud, Margaret Mead, Virginia Woolf, and Jane Fonda to illustrate their points.

Constructing the Multigenerational Family Genogram: Exploring a Problem in Context. Available for rental or sale through Menninger Video Productions, Box 829, Topeka, KS 66601, 1–800–345–6036. This video illustrates the construction and use of the multigenerational family genogram. A detailed case vignette highlights the important areas of information a genogram can provide.

Notes

Chapter 1   The Pursuit of Intimacy: Is It Women's Work?

5   On the impact of marriage on women's mental health see E. Carmen, N. F. Russo, and J. B. Miller, "Inequality and Women's Mental Health," in the *American Journal of Psychiatry* 138/10 (1981): 1319–1330, which also appears in P. Reiker and E. Carmen, eds., *The Gender Gap in Psychotherapy* (New York: Coward McCann, 1983). Also see Jessie Bernard, *The Future of Marriage*, 2nd edition, (New Haven: Yale University Press, 1982) and M. Walters, B. Carter, P. Papp, and O. Silverstein, *The Invisible Web: Gender Patterns in Family Relationships* (New York: Guilford Press, 1988).

5–7   See Jean Baker Miller, *Toward a New Psychology of Women* (Boston: Beacon Press, 1986), for an appreciation of the complex links between women's relationship orientation and women's subordinate group status. Miller's pioneering work has inspired new psychoanalytic perspectives on women's investment in connectedness and relatedness. See *The Stone Center Working Papers* on women (The Stone Center, Wellesley College, Wellesley, MA 02181). Also see Carol Gilligan, *In a Different Voice* (Cambridge: Harvard University Press, 1982).

Chapter 2   The Challenge of Change

PAGE

10   The story of the New England farmer (and related insights about the quest for personal growth) is from Robert J. McAllister, *Living the Vows* (San Francisco: Harper & Row, 1986), pp. 127–143.

11   On the subject of change (and resistance to change in families) see Peggy Papp, *The Process of Change* (New York: Guilford Press, 1983).

Chapter 3   Selfhood: At What Cost?

22   "Letter to the Editor," *Ms.* magazine, September 1980.

23–25   More about women's compromised and de-selfed position in marriage and with men can be found in H. G. Lerner, *The Dance of Anger* (New York: Harper & Row, 1985), chapter 2. Also see H. G. Lerner, *Women in Therapy*, (Northvale, NJ: Jason Aronson, 1988; paperback edition from Harper & Row, 1989), chapters 11 and 13.

See also Paula Kaplan, *The Myth of Women's Masochism*, (New York: E. P. Dutton, 1984).

31–33   Traditional psychoanalytic concepts of self and theories regarding dependency and autonomy in women continue to be re-examined and revised by feminist theorists such as Jean Baker Miller and the work of the Stone Center, *op. cit.* See also Lerner, *op. cit,* 1988, Gilligan, *op. cit.,* 1982, Luise Eichenbaum and Susie Orbach, *What Do Women Want* (New York: Coward McCann, 1983), and Nancy Chodorow, *The Reproduction of Mothering* (Berkeley: University of California Press, 1978).

The concept of self and the complex interplay between separateness and connectedness have been most

PAGE

fully elaborated in psychoanalytic theory and Bowen family systems theory. For a comprehensive review of Bowen theory see Michael Kerr, "Family Systems Theory and Therapy," in Alan Gurman and David Knistern, eds., *Handbook of Family Therapy* (New York: Brunner/Mazel, 1981), pp. 226–64 and Michael Kerr, "Chronic Anxiety and Defining a Self," *The Atlantic Monthly* 262/3 (September 1988): 35–58. Also see Michael Kerr and Murray Bowen, *Family Evaluation* (New York: Norton, 1988).

Bowen family systems theory differs from other systemic approaches in its attempts to root theory in evolutionary biology rather than general systems theory. Because the writings of Bowen and his colleagues are singularly male-centered in language and worldview, it may be difficult to appreciate the value of Bowen's ideas for the psychotherapy of women. For a feminist critique of Bowen theory see Deborah A. Luepnitz, *The Family Interpreted: Feminist Theory in Clinical Practice* (New York: Basic Books, Inc., 1988), chapter 3, pp. 36–47. For the clinical application of Bowen's ideas by a feminist therapist see Lerner, *op. cit.*, 1988, chapters 12 and 13 and H. G. Lerner, "The Challenge of Change" in Carol Tavris, ed., *Everywoman's Emotional Well-being* (New York: Doubleday & Company, 1986), chapter 18.

34   Overfunctioning-underfunctioning reciprocity, fighting, distancing, and child-focus have been described at length in the family systems literature as ways of managing anxiety and navigating relationships under stress. See Murray Bowen, *Family Therapy in Clinical Practice* (New York: Jason Aronson, 1978), Kerr, *op. cit.*, 1981, and Kerr and Bowen, *op. cit.*, 1988.

Chapter 4   Anxiety Revisited: Naming the Problem

37   The pattern of pursuit and distance has been widely described in the family therapy literature. See Phillip Guerin

and Katherine Buckley Guerin, "Theoretical Aspects and Clinical Relevance of the Multigenerational Model of Family Therapy," in Philip Guerin, ed., *Family Therapy* (New York: Gardner Press, 1976), pp. 91–110.

On breaking the pursuit cycle see the example of Sandra and Larry, chapter 3, in Lerner, *op. cit.*, 1985.

46   Most therapeutic approaches strive for the reduction of anxiety and the awareness of its sources. On the impact of anxiety moving down and across generations see Betty Carter and Monica McGoldrick, "Overview: The Changing Family Life Cycle," in Betty Carter and Monica McGoldrick, eds., *The Changing Family Life Cycle: A Framework for Family Therapy,* 2nd edition, (New York: Gardner Press, 1988), pp. 8–9. Also see Betty Carter, "The Transgenerational Scripts and Nuclear Family Stress: Theory and Clinical Implications," in R. R. Sager, ed., *Georgetown Family Symposium* 3 (Washington, D.C.: Georgetown University, 1975–76).

Chapter 5   Distance and More Distance

54   I am grateful to the well-developed theoretical insights of Murray Bowen regarding distance and cutoff from nuclear and extended family.

Chapter 6   Dealing with Differences

73–75   My interest in ethnicity in the therapeutic process was sparked by a workshop conducted by family therapist Monica McGoldrick, whose teachings are reflected in this clinical example. Also see Monica McGoldrick, J. K.

Pearce, and J. Giordano, *Ethnicity and Family Therapy* (New York: Guilford Press, 1982) and Monica McGoldrick and N. Garcia Preto, "Ethnic Intermarriage: Implications for Therapy," *Family Process* 23/3 (1984): 347–364.

80   Reactivity should not be confused with effectively voiced anger that serves to challenge the status quo and preserve the dignity and integrity of the self. On the importance of female anger and protest see Teresa Bernardez-Bonesatti, "Women and Anger: Conflicts with Aggression in Contemporary Women," in the *Journal of the American Medical Women's Association* 33 (1978): 215–19. For a comprehensive overview on anger see Carol Tavris, *Anger: The Misunderstood Emotion* (New York: Simon & Schuster, 1982).

81–85 Marla Beth Isaacs, Braulio Montalvo, and David Abelsohn have written a useful book for therapists (and others involved in the divorce process) to help divorcing parents move out of intense, child-focused triangles toward more functional parenting. See *The Difficult Divorce* (New York: Basic Books, Inc., 1986).

Chapter 8   Understanding Overfunctioning

102   I am grateful to Katherine Glenn Kent for helping me to appreciate the fine points of the overfunctioning-underfunctioning reciprocity in my clinical work. More on this subject can be found in Bowen, *op. cit.*, 1978, Kerr, *op. cit.*, 1981, and Kerr and Bowen, *op. cit.*, 1988.

108–12 On modifying an overfunctioning-underfunctioning pattern see the example of Lois and her brother in Lerner, *op. cit.*, 1985, chapter 4.

Family therapist Marianne Ault-Riché has co-produced an educational videotape describing her attempts to modify her overfunctioning position in her family of origin. See *Love and Work: One Woman's Study of Her Family of Origin,* (Menninger Video Productions, The Menninger Foundation, Box 829, Topeka, KS 66601).

113   Part of this case example was previously published by H. G. Lerner, "Get Yourself Unstuck from Mom," in *Working Mother,* December 1986, pp. 64–72.

Chapter 9   Very Hot Issues: A Process View of Change

123   Lyrics by Jo-Ann Krestan from the musical *Elizabeth Rex or The Well-Bred Mother Goes to Camp.* Produced by the Broadway-Times Theatre Co. New York City, December 1983. Used by permission.

On a daughter's disclosure of lesbianism to her mother see Jo-Ann Krestan, "Lesbian Daughters and Lesbian Mothers: The Crisis of Disclosure from a Family Systems Perspective," in Lois Braverman, ed., *Women, Feminism, and Family Therapy* (New York: The Haworth Press, 1988).

125   On the costs of secrecy for the lesbian couple see Jo-Ann Krestan and Claudia Bepko, "The Problem of Fusion in the Lesbian Relationship," *Family Process* 19 (1980): 277–289.

137–38   I am indebted to Sallyann Roth and Bianca Cody Murphy for these and other questions and for their lucid work on systematic questioning with lesbian clients. See Sallyann Roth and Bianca Cody, "Therapeutic Work with Lesbian Clients: A Systemic Therapy View," in M. Ault-Riché, ed., *Women and Family Therapy* (Rockville, MD: Aspen Systems Corporation, 1986), pp. 78–89.

Chapter 10   Tackling Triangles

143   Triangles are a key concept in most family systems approaches. I am grateful to the teachings of Katherine
Glenn Kent on triangles in family and work systems.

For a comprehensive review of triangles within marriage and the family see Philip Guerin, L. Fay, S. Burden,
and J. Gilbert Kautto, *The Evaluation and Treatment of
Marital Conflict* (New York: Basic Books, 1987). Also see
Kerr, *op. cit.*, 1981 and Kerr and Bowen, *op. cit.*, 1988.

Chapter 11   Bold New Moves: The Story of Linda

162   For a detailed description of moving out of a child-
focused triangle, see Lerner, *op. cit.*, 1985, chapter 8. Also
see Maggie Scarf, *Intimate Partners* (New York: Random
House, 1987).

Chapter 12   Our Mother/Her Mother/Our Self

184   Part of this case example appeared in Lerner, "Get Unstuck from Mom," *op. cit.*, 1986.

For more on the subject of navigating separateness and
connectedness in the mother-daughter relationship see
Lerner, *op. cit.*, 1985, chapter 4. Also see Lerner, *op. cit.*,
1988.

186   Mother-blaming and a narrow mother-focused view of
family problems still characterize both psychoanalytic and
family systems theory and therapy. See Nancy Chodorow
and S. Contratto's "The Fantasy of the Perfect Mother,"
in B. Thorne and M. Yalom, eds., *Rethinking the Family:*

Some Feminist Questions (New York: Longman, 1982), pp. 54–75. Also see Lerner, *op. cit.*, 1988, pp. 255–285 and Evan Imber Black, "Women, Families, and Larger Systems," in Ault-Riché, ed., *op. cit.*, 1986, pp 25–33.

See also Adrienne Rich, *Of Woman Born* (New York: W. W. Norton, 1976), Lois Braverman, "Beyond the Myth of Motherhood," in Monica McGoldrick, C. M. Anderson, and F. Walsh, eds., *Women in Families* (New York: W. W. Norton, 1989), chapter 12, Luepnitz, *op. cit.*, 1988, and Walters, Carter, Papp, and Silverstein, *op. cit.*, 1988.

187   Thanks to Rachel Hare-Mustin, a pioneer in feminist family therapy, for her quote on women's guilt.

187   Psychoanalytic theory has tended to "pathologize" the mother-daughter dyad, focusing narrowly on the darker side of separation struggles in this relationship. For new psychoanalytic contributions that challenge traditional views see J. V. Jordon and J. L. Surrey, "The Self-in-Relation: Empathy and the Mother-Daughter Relationship," in T. Bernay and D. W. Cantor, eds., *The Psychology of Today's Woman* (Hillsdale, NJ: The Analytic Press, 1986), pp. 81–104. Also see J. L. Herman and H. B. Lewis, "Anger in the Mother-Daughter Relationship," in Bernay and Cantor, eds., *op. cit.*, 1986, pp. 139–168.

Chapter 13   Reviewing Self-Focus: The Foundations of Intimacy

209   Communicating from a self-focused position requires the ability to take an "I" position on important issues. Thomas Gordon, founder of Parent Effectiveness Training has done pioneering work on "I" messages. His book *Parent Effectiveness Training* (New York: New American Library, 1975) is a useful model of self-focused communication for all relationships. See also Lerner, *op. cit.*, 1985, chapter 5.

216–17   Bowen theory and therapy are especially useful in gaining a broader, more objective perspective on the emotional process (including cutoffs and triangles) in one's own family and working to gradually modify one's own part in the patterns that block growth.

        The adoption experience is an example of a particularly intense cutoff where the adoptee's inquiry and search for birth parents may consciously or unconsciously be experienced as a disloyalty, threat, or betrayal. See Betty Jean Lifton, *Lost and Found: The Adoption Experience* (New York: Harper & Row, 1988) and *Twice Born: Memoirs of an Adopted Daughter* (New York: Penguin Books, 1977). As a rule, any significant cutoff from a key family member binds intense underground anxiety and emotionality that may hit one like a ton of bricks during (and not until) the process of re-connecting.

218   While the importance of a life plan for women may seem more than obvious, I am grateful to Betty Carter and Katherine Glenn Kent for their insightful thoughts on the subject.

        A life plan is crucial for women, not only because of our special vulnerability to poverty, but also because economic dependence on a man impedes or precludes the process of defining the self and taking a bottom-line position in that relationship. See Lerner, *op. cit.*, 1988, pp. 243–246 and Walters, Carter, Papp, and Silverstein, *op. cit.*, 1988.

Epilogue

223   Any attempt to understand, diagnose, or treat human problems apart from the socio-political context (including the profound impact of gender-determined family and work roles) is necessarily problematic. For a provocative commentary on current psychiatric diagnosis see Matthew P. Dumont, "A Diagnostic Parable (First Edition–Unre-

vised)," in *Readings: A Journal of Reviews and Commentary in Mental Health* 2/4 (December 1987): 9–12.

223–24   Feminist psychoanalytic thinkers have long challenged and revised traditional phallocentric views on female psychology, and they continue to do so. Only recently are family systems thinkers re-examining theory and practice from a feminist perspective. See McGoldrick, Anderson, and Walsh, eds., *op. cit.*, 1989, chapter 1, for a brief history of feminist contributions to the family therapy field. Also see Judith Myers Avis, "Deepening Awareness: A Private Study Guide to Feminism and Family Therapy," in Braverman, *op. cit.*, 1987, pp. 15–46 and Walters, Carter, Papp, and Silverstein, *op. cit.*, 1988.

To raise one's consciousness and to keep current on ideas and issues central to women's lives I recommend subscribing to *New Directions for Women* (published since 1972), 108 West Palisade Avenue, Englewood, NJ 07631.

Index

Adrienne, 206
  distancing and, 52–69
    from brother, 56, 57, 62–64
    from father, 56–67
    mother and, 64–66
  hot topics and, 127
  triangles and, 54, 143
Adult Children of Alcoholics, 91,
  99
Adultery. *See* Extramarital affairs
Advice, giving, 104, 115, 117,
  119, 120, 168, 189
Affairs. *See* Extramarital affairs
Aging parents, 116–17
  care of, 72–74
Alcoholism
  defining a bottom line and, 87–
    101
  overfunctioning and, 110–12
Ambivalent partners, 40, 43–45
Anger, 13, 18, 26, 45, 48, 65, 71,
    83–85, 90, 93, 97, 109,
    118, 140
  repressed, 96, 111–12
  triangles and, 145
Anglo-Saxon Protestant families,
    73, 74
Anita and Helen, overfunctioning
    and, 113–21
Anne. *See* Cathy and Anne

Anniversaries
  anxiety and, 48–50
  triangles and, 144
Anxiety, 9, 13, 33–51
  anniversaries and, 48–50
  avoiding, 36
  bottom line and, 43–45
  change and, 13, 16–18, 27, 129
  difference and, 71
  distancing and, 89. *See also*
    Cutoff
  emotional field and, 46–48, 89,
    92
  illness and, 28–30
  intensity (intense feelings) and,
    63–64
  managing. *See* Stress
    management
  of men, 8, 29, 33–34
  pursuit cycle and, 37–45
  reactivity and, 36–38, 43, 47,
    114
  seeking distance and, 53
  sources of, 45–50
  stuck relationships and, 34–36,
    122
  triangles and, 148–49, 151–55,
    157–60, 162–64
Approval, intimacy vs. winning, 7
Assertiveness, 163, 193

Attachment, 2, 7, 54, 64
Attraction of opposites, 76, 83
Autonomy, 19, 31

Beliefs, 209, 211
  clarification of, 220
  difference and, 71, 85
Ben, learning and change of,
    15–16
Betrayal, 25, 143–44
Bill, Sue, and Willy, child-focused
    triangle of, 154–56
Blacks, 6, 155
Blaming, 48, 68, 87–101, 134, 152
  mother-daughter relationship
    and, 183, 186–87, 190
  overfunctioning and, 102
  of self, 27, 207
  triangles and, 155, 156, 163, 177
Bottom line, 43–45, 90–97, 177,
    210
  defining of, 90–92
  fallout from establishment of,
    93–97
  lack of, 95–96
  "tests" and countermoves and,
    92–93, 97
Boundaries. See Limits
Bowen, Murray, 232
  family systems theory, 105
Brazelton, Thomas B., 223

Cancer, 28–30, 56–57, 60–61, 206
Career goals, 39, 41, 220
Career issues, 66
  avoiding, 57, 58
Cathy and Anne, mother-daughter
    relationship of, 184–98
  difference and, 188–93
  hot topics and, 193–97
  mother-guilt and, 186–88
Change(s), behavioral
  anxiety and, 129
  blowing it and, 110
  challenge of, 10–19
  conservative policy for, 11–16

Change(s) (cont.)
  costs of, 23–24
  courage and, 27, 48
  fallout from, 64–67
  fear of, 10–11
  guidelines for, 3–4
  inevitability of, 16
  overfunctioning and, 108–13
  partner. See Partner change
  problems and, 12–14, 17–18,
    27–28
  reasons for, 10–11
  resistance to, 23–30
  sameness vs., 11, 15–16
  in short run vs. long run, 9
  small, 14–15
  social and political change and,
    224
  stuck relationships and, 16–
    19
  timing of, 99
  will to, 10–11
"Change back!" reactions, 193
Child-focus, 51, 80
  difference and, 82–85
  stress management and, 13–14,
    29–30, 34, 37, 50
  triangles and, 154–60
Children
  birth of, 52, 56, 57
  focus on needs of, 156
  other-focus of, 147
  triangles and, 146–51, 154–
    60
Claire. See Linda, Claire, and
    mother
Codependency, 98
Coming out, 124–28, 141–42
Commitment, 37–43
  ambivalence and, 40–43
Communication, 3, 8, 100, 119,
    202, 212–13. See also Hot
    topics
  avoiding, 57, 60, 61
  hot topics and, 124, 128, 130
  mixed messages and, 20–21

Communication *(cont.)*
    process view of change and, 140
    triangles and, 173–74
    unconscious, 20–21
Competence, 81–84, 99, 117,
    119, 201
    relating to, 109, 112, 120–21,
        177
Conflict, 2, 151. *See also* Fighting
Connectedness, 2, 35, 41, 100,
    179, 211–12
    anxiety and, 53
    defining a bottom line and, 97–
        98
    of men, 7
    need for, 71
    self-development and, 9
    self-focus and, 212–14
    triangles and, 145, 172–74
Conservative policy for change,
    11–16
*Constructing the Multigenerational
    Family Genogram: Exploring
    a Problem in Context,* 233
Courage, 59, 110, 173, 180, 207
    change and, 27, 48
    process view of change and,
        125–26
Criticism
    mother-daughter relationship
        and, 185, 187, 189
    triangles and, 145
Crying, 61, 119, 129, 206
Cultural differences, 73–80, 86
Cutoff, 48, 53, 55, 86, 97–98,
    212, 213
    in first family, 56–57, 59, 65
    as managing anxiety, 63
    process view of change and,
        133, 140

Dance of Anger, The (Lerner), 202,
    204
"Daughter's Song, The" (Krestan),
    123

David and Susan, pursuit cycle
    and, 37–42, 46, 50–51,
    121–22
Death, 38
    of fathers, 60–62
    of grandparents, 13, 18, 47
    of mothers, 48, 49
    stress management and, 28–30
Depression, 27, 49, 80, 89, 209–11
    attempt to change
        overfunctioning and, 107,
        109, 111
    fear of, 130
    in men, 13, 25
    of mothers, 64, 65
    triangles and, 162, 167, 175,
        178, 180–82
De-selfing, 105–8
Differences, 35, 70–101, 202
    anxiety and, 71
    child-focus and, 82–85
    ethnicity and, 73–80, 86
    filters and, 71, 75
    first families and, 72–79
    generalizations, 75–76
    growth and, 71
    hot topics and, 126
    intensity and, 72
    mother-daughter relationship
        and, 188–93
    opposites attract and, 76, 83
    as problem, 73, 83–85
    reactivity and, 72, 76, 80–86,
        114
    self-focus and, 77–78
    stress management and, 79–80
    as taboo, 25
    as threat, 32
Distance, 18, 52–69, 115. *See also*
        Anxiety; Conflict; Cutoff;
        Fighting
    as alternative to
        overfunctioning, 112
    anxiety and, 89
    emotional field and, 55–58
    in fathers, 14, 29, 57, 60–62, 80

Distance *(cont.)*
illness and, 56–57, 60–62
intensity and, 17, 34, 54, 55, 63
intimacy vs., 1, 2
in marriage, 52–59, 67–69
men and, 8, 14, 29, 33–34, 37–
45, 80
mother-daughter relationship
and, 183–84, 189
need for, 16
overfunctioning and, 118
as problem or solution, 53–67
process view of change and, 132
stress management and, 29, 33–
34, 37, 48, 50, 53–55, 57–
58, 89–90, 121–22
too much, 17, 18
triangles and, 145–46, 163
Divorce, 49, 80, 95, 185, 189
emotionally married vs., 81–86
Dominance, 32
Dominant groups, subordinate
groups compared, 6, 7
Dorothy and father, process view
of change and, 136
Dyads, 142, 151

Economic dependence, 24–25
Economic security, 219–20
Elaine and Adrienne
fallout from change and, 64–66
mother-guilt and, 187
Eleanor, self-focus and, 217
Emotional field
anxiety and, 46–48, 89, 92
distancing and, 55–58
Emotional maturity, 105
Emotions. *See* Feelings
Energy, use of, 115–16
Ethnicity, differences and, 73–80,
86, 155
Exhaustion, 118
Expert advice, limits of, 26–27,
30–31

Extramarital affairs, 59, 143–44
discovery of, 52, 54
protective function of, 54, 55

Family, 184, 189, 214–15
anniversaries and, 49–50
cutoff in, 56–57, 59, 65
defining a bottom line and, 87–
101
difference and, 72–73
history of "second sons" in, 56,
57
hot topics and, 130
marital problems affected by,
56–57, 59
romantic relationships and, 38–
40, 46–47
stress management in, 13–14,
28–30, 33–34
triangles and, 145–46
view of reality determined by, 71
Family diagrams. *See* Genograms
Family systems therapy, 39,
217–18
Fathers, 8, 9, 13
alcoholism of, 87–101, 110–12
death of, 60–62
distancing and, 14, 29, 33–34,
57, 60, 80
illness of, 38, 56–57, 60–62, 80
process view of change and, 136
self-focus and, 217
Feedback, 168, 174, 185, 209
Feelings. *See also specific feelings*
intense. *See* Intensity
of powerlessness, 223–24
reactivity vs., 205–6
self-focus and, 203–6
venting of, 204–5
Feminism, 108, 156, 207–8
Fighting, 34, 37, 48, 50, 95, 155
marital, 52, 53, 56, 58
mother-daughter relationship
and, 190
Fight-or-flight response, 53

Filters, different, 71, 75
"Finding somebody," as women's
    job, 5, 6
Firstborns, overfunctioning and,
    28, 103
"Fix-it" mode, 79
Flirtation, serious, 54, 55, 57
Frances. *See* Lois and Frances
Frank and Adrienne. *See also*
    Adrienne
    distancing and marriage of, 52–
        59, 67–69
    triangles and, 54, 143
Frustration, 118
Fusion, 53

Gender roles, 78–79
Genograms, 199–200, 214–15,
    224
    bibliographical information on,
        232–33
    creating, 225–26
    symbols for, 226–29
Genograms in Family Assessment
    (McGoldrick and Gerson),
    232–33
Gerson, Randy, 232–33
Gossip, 152–54
    triangles and, 164
Grandparents, 96, 196
    death of, 13, 18, 47
    overfunctioning and, 113–21
Greg and Adrienne
    distancing and, 56, 62–67
    hot topics and, 127
Grief, 48
Group therapy, 87–88, 91, 99, 110
Growth, difference and, 71
Guilt, 65–67, 97, 156, 196
    difference and, 72–73
    good reasons for, 67
    incest and, 134–35
    mother, 186–88

Hank. *See* Jo-Anne and Hank
Heather and Ira, emotional field
    and, 46–47
Helen. *See* Anita and Helen
Hot topics, 122–42
    difference and, 126
    incest, 133–35, 137
    lesbianism, 124–28, 137–42
    mother-daughter relationship
        and, 193–97
    suicide and depression, 130
    types of, 127
Humility, self-focus and, 208–9
Husbands
    resistance to change and, 23–27
    wife's selfhood resisted by,
        22–27
    wives' accommodating of, 25

Identity, 16, 25
    lesbian, 125
"I" language, 91, 174, 177
Illness
    anxiety and, 28–30
    distancing and, 56–57, 60–62
    of fathers, 38, 56–57, 60–62, 80
    of mothers, 48
Incest, 47
    process view of change and,
        127, 133–35, 137
Incompetence, 81
Independence, 19, 20, 22, 31–32,
    105
    mother-daughter relationship
        and, 187–88
Individuality, 74
Infidelity. *See* Extramarital affairs
In-law triangles, 144–51
Insight, 40, 57–58
Intensity (intense feelings), 43,
    63–64
    difference and, 72
    distancing and, 17, 34, 54, 55,
        63

Intensity *(cont.)*
    intimacy vs., 2
    reactivity and, 84–85, 93
    sameness vs., 70
    sources of, 47–48
    too much, 17, 18
    triangles and, 144–45, 149–50,
        167–68
Intimacy (intimate relationships).
    See also specific topics
    definition of, 1–3
    goal of, 4, 201–2
    importance of, 211–12
    what it is not, 1–2
Ira. *See* Heather and Ira
Irresponsibility, 89
Isolation, 16, 71, 148
Italian families, 73–74, 76

Janine, self-focus and, 212–13
Jo-Anne and Hank
    hot topics and, 127
    overfunctioning vs.
        underfunctioning and,
        105–8
    resistance to change and, 23–27,
        219
    selfhood scale and, 32–33
Joe, birth of, 56, 57
John. *See* Suzanne and John
Judy, "problem" behavior of, 13–
    14, 28
Julie
    Emma, Rob, and, triangles and,
        146–48, 151
    Shirley, Emma, and, in-law
        triangles and, 148–50
    Shirley, Rob, and, in-law
        triangles and, 144–46, 148,
        150, 151
June and Tom, difference and,
    81–85

Kimberly, process view of change
    and, 124–28, 131–32, 137–
    42

Kramer vs. Kramer, 156
Krestan, Jo-Ann, 123
Kristen
    changes in overfunctioning and,
        108–12
    defining a bottom line and, 87–
        101

Learning, difference and, 71
Lesbianism, 131–32, 187
    process view of change and,
        124–28, 137–42
Life plans, 218–21
Life-styles, difference and, 82–83
Limits
    clarification of, 3, 45, 175–77.
        See also Bottom line
    establishing, 78
Linda, Claire, and mother,
        triangles and, 162–82
    connecting with Claire and,
        172–74
    emotion vs. reactivity and, 206
    getting off Claire and, 167–68
    getting out of the middle and,
        166–67
    limit setting and, 175–77
    men and, 162, 178–79
    sharing underfunctioning
        and, 177–78
    sharing reactions and, 174
    tests and, 169–72
    tracking the triangle and,
        163–66
Lois and Frances, emotional field
    and, 48
Long-term relationships, intimacy
    and, 2
Love, 63–64, 211. *See also*
    Romantic encounters
    traditional, 5

McGoldrick, Monica, 232–33
Male culture, 6–7, 223
Margie, process view of change
    and, 129–31

Marriage, 2, 219
  distance in, 52–59, 67–69
  emotional, divorce vs., 81–86
  fighting in, 52, 53, 56, 58
  in-law triangles and, 144–51
  overloading of, 56–59, 62
  reciprocal (or circular)
    relationship pattern in,
    105–8
  relationship work in, 8
  traditional, 5, 8
Marsha, self-focus and, 216–17
Mary and Kimberly, 124–25
Matthew, Steve, and author, child-
  focused triangle of, 157–60
Maturity, 193
Mead, Margaret, 27
Men, 2. See also Fathers; Husbands
  anxiety of, 8, 29, 33–34
  connectedness of, 7
  depression in, 13, 25
  distancing and, 8, 14, 29,
    33–34, 80
  fears of, 154, 155
  pseudo-independence of, 32
  relationship needs of, 4
  relationship work as minor
    concern of, 5, 7–9
Mother-daughter relationship,
  183–200
  blaming and, 183, 186–87
  defining a bottom line and, 93–
    98
  difference and, 188–93
  distancing and, 57, 58, 60, 61,
    64–66, 183–84, 189
  hot topics and, 124–25,
    129–32, 193–97
  overfunctioning and, 113–21
  reactivity and, 183–84, 186
  separateness and, 183–84, 187–
    88, 191–92
  triangles and, 146–48, 151,
    162–82, 185, 188
Mother-guilt, 186–88

Mother-in-laws, triangles and,
  144–46, 148–50
Mothers, 13, 61. See also Mother-
  daughter relationship
  death of, 48
  defining a bottom line and, 89–
    99
  depression of, 64, 65
  distance and, 57, 58, 60, 61,
    64–66
  illness of, 28–30, 48
  as middlemen, 57, 58, 60
  overfunctioning and, 113–21
  process view of change and,
    124–25, 129–32
  selfhood of, 30, 34, 184, 198
  triangles and, 146–48
"Mother's Song, The" (Kresten),
  123
Mourning, 62
Ms. magazine, 22, 24, 26, 27, 32,
  219

Negative traits, positive aspects of,
  11–14

Only children, overfunctioning
  and, 103
Other-focus, 59, 72, 95, 121, 180,
  206–7, 209–11. See also
  Child-focus
  anxiety and, 34, 37–39
  children and, 147
  overfunctioning and, 104, 116–
    17
  reactivity and, 87–88, 90, 95
  stress management and, 104
Overfunctioning, 28–30, 33, 34,
  37, 81–83, 95, 100–22,
  130, 209, 211
  advantages of, 116–17
  alternative behavior to, 117–18
  birth order and, 28, 103
  characteristics of, 104
  chronic, 113
  collapse and, 104

Overfunctioning *(cont.)*
  costs of, 112
  definition of, 104
  mild, 113–21
  nonproblematic vs. problematic,
      103
  reciprocal (or circular)
      relationship pattern and,
      105–8
  sharing vs., 170
  as stress management, 90, 103,
      104, 121
  stuck relationships and, 103,
      105, 109, 120
  triangles and, 166–67
  underfunctioning vs., 100–2,
      115
  will to change and, 108–13

Pain, 109
Painful issues, 35
Panic, 38, 49, 63
Parents. *See also* Fathers; Mothers
  aging, 72–74, 116–17
  expectations of, 7–8
  hot topics and, 124–28
Partner change
  impossibility of, 7, 88
  resistance to, 22–27
Perspective, 51, 71, 79, 209
Pseudo-self, 105–8
Plans
  life, 218–21
  stress management and, 40–42
Political change, 224
Powerlessness, feelings of, 223–24
Problems, 48
  context of, 24–26
  determining, 17–18, 50–51
  differences as, 73, 83–85
  outcome of high anxiety vs., 50
  purpose of, 12–14, 27–28
  reactivity as, 84, 85
  timing of, 38
Problem solving, 37, 58, 117
  misguided, 13, 14

Problem solving *(cont.)*
  overfunctioning and, 104
  plans and, 40–42
  reactivity and, 88–89
Process view of change, 123–42
  coming out and, 124–28,
      141–42
  countermoves and, 129–31
  feelings as guide in, 140–41
  laying the groundwork and,
      132–33
  resistance from within and,
      131–33
  return to the source and,
      135–37
  speed of, 133–36
  timing and, 139–40
Protective behavior, 219
  extramarital affair as, 54, 55
Protectiveness, sensitivity vs., 61
Pseudo-independence, 31–32
Pursuing (pursuit cycle), 34, 68
  anxiety and, 37–45
  breaking of, 40–41
  negative effects, 59

Questioning, 61
  process view of change and,
      137–38
  triangles and, 173–74

Rage. *See* Anger
Rayna and brother, process view
      of change and, 133–35, 137
Reactions, sharing of, 174
Reactivity, 40, 41, 43, 48, 87–90,
      110, 180
  anniversaries and, 49
  anxiety and, 36–38, 43, 47, 114
  avoiding, 44–45
  child-focused triangles and,
      157–60
  difference and, 72, 76, 80–86,
      114
  emotionality vs., 205–6

Reactivity *(cont.)*
   intensity (intense feelings) and,
      84–85, 93
   mother-daughter relationship
      and, 183–84, 186
   other-focus and, 87–88, 90, 95
   overt vs. covert, 90
   as problem, 84, 85
   process view of change and,
      137–42
   self-focus and, 211–12
   stuck relationships and, 80–81,
      90
   thinking vs., 137–42
   toning down, 86. *See also*
      Bottom line
Reality, 96
   challenging of view of, 111
   male defining of, 223
Reciprocal (or circular)
   relationship pattern, 105–8
Relationships, 7. *See also* Intimacy;
     Marriage; *and specific topics*
   between dominant and
     subordinate groups, 6
   dyads, 142, 151
   emotional tone in, 204
   long-term. *See* Long-term
     relationships
   male vs. female need for, 4–5
   mother-daughter. *See* Mother-
     daughter relationship
   overloading of, 39
   romantic. *See* Romantic
     encounters
   sibling. *See* Sibling relationships
   stuck. *See* Stuck relationships
   triangles. *See* Triangles
Relationship work
   men's lack of concern about, 5,
     7–9
   as women's work, 4–9
Religion, self-focus and, 212–13
Resistance, process view of change
   and, 126, 131–33

Responsibility, 78, 99, 134
   family and, 74
   stress management and, 79, 81–
     82
   triangles and, 151, 167, 177
Retarded brothers, distancing
   and, 56, 57, 62–67
Rob. *See* Julie, Emma, and Rob;
     Julie, Shirley, and Rob
Romantic encounters, 1, 2, 162,
   178–79
   family's effects on, 38–40,
     46–47
   pursuit cycle and, 37–42

Sameness
   change vs., 11, 15–16
   intensity (intense feelings) vs., 70
Schizophrenia, 89
Self-blame, 27, 207
Self-esteem, 7
   low, 27, 134
Self-focus, 39, 86, 163, 180, 201–
   22
   being a self and, 209–11
   bottom-line position and, 95,
     99–101
   connectedness and, 212–14
   difference and, 77–78
   emotional separateness and,
     211–14
   feelings and, 203–6
   humility and, 208–9
   life-plans and, 218–21
   process view of change and,
     138–40
   timing and, 215–18
   triangles and, 155, 157–60
   understanding, 206–14
Self-hatred, 27
Self-help books, 4
   how to use, 202–3
Selfhood, 3. *See also* Separateness
   connectedness and, 9
   defining of, 190–93, 209–11
   de-selfing and, 105–8

Selfhood *(cont.)*
    as dilemma for women, 21–22
    importance of, 18–19
    insufficient, 53
    of men vs. women, 7, 21–22
    mixed messages and, 20–21
    mother-daughter relationship
        and, 190–93
    of mothers, 30, 34, 184, 198
    need for, 34–35
    overfunctioning vs.
        underfunctioning and,
        100–1, 105–8
    problem solving and, 18–19
    pseudo-, 32, 105–8
    relationship overloading vs., 39
    scale of, 31–35
    success and, 31–32
    true (solid), 105–6, 163
    of wives, husband's resistance
        of, 22–27
    working on, 68–69
Selfishness, 110
Self-reliance, 74, 76
Sensitivity, protectiveness vs., 61
Separateness, 2, 3, 9, 19, 22, 41.
    See also Selfhood
    mother-daughter relationship
        and, 183, 187–88, 191–92
    self-focus and, 211–14
    triangles and, 145
Sexual abuse, 48
Sharing
    overfunctioning vs., 170
    reactions, 174
    underfunctioning, 177–78
Shirley. *See* Julie, Shirley, and
        Emma; Julie, Shirley, and
        Rob
Sibling relationships
    anxiety and, 48
    distancing and, 56, 57, 62–67
    process view of change and,
        139, 140
Social change, 224

Spock, Benjamin, 223
Status, 6, 7, 82
Steve. *See* Matthew, Steve, and
        author
Strauss Family Genogram, 231–32
Strengths, 35
    weaknesses vs., 11–12, 100-1
Stress management, 13–14,
        28–30, 33–34, 37, 50, 202.
        See also Triangles
    child-focus as, 13–14, 37
    death and, 28–30
    difference and, 79–80
    distancing as, 53–55, 57–58,
        89–90, 121–22
    fighting as, 34, 37, 48
    overfunctioning as, 28–30, 33,
        34, 37, 81–83, 90, 103,
        104, 121
    plans and, 40–42
    pursuit cycle and, 37–42
    underfunctioning as, 28–30, 33,
        34, 37, 82, 83, 103, 121
Stuck relationships, 16–19, 48
    anxiety and, 34–36, 122
    mother-daughter relationship
        and, 183
    overfunctioning and, 103, 105,
        109, 120
    polarities and, 39
    reactivity and, 80–81, 90
Subordinate groups
    dominant groups compared
        with, 6, 7
    selfhood and, 21
Success, selfhood and, 31–32
Sue. *See* Bill, Sue, and Willy
Suicidal fantasies, 64
Suicide, 130, 173, 175, 176
Susan
    overfunctioning and, 121
    overfunctioning of, 28–30, 33
    pursuit cycle and, 37–42, 46,
        50–51, 121–22
Suzanne and John, 72–79, 86, 114

Symptomatic spouse, 50

Therapist, triangles and, 152
Thinking, 159
  about feelings, 203–6
  reactivity vs., 137–42
Togetherness, 79. *See also*
      Connectedness
  Italian families and, 74, 76
Tom. *See* June and Tom
Triangles, 89–90, 142–82. *See also*
      Extramarital affairs
  anniversaries and, 144
  anxiety and, 148–49, 151, 152–
      53, 154–55, 157–60, 162–
      64
  child-focused, 82–85, 154–60
    at societal level, 155–56
  communication and, 173–74
  connectedness and, 172–74
  definition of, 151–52
  distancing and, 145–46
  gossip and, 152–54, 164
  in-law, 144–51
  intensity and, 144–45, 149–50,
      167–68
  mother-daughter relationship
      and, 185, 188
  protective function of, 54, 55
  stability of, 154
"True" or "solid" self, level of,
      105–6
Tunnel vision, 50–51

Unconscious, 30, 31, 57, 65
  guilt and, 66
Unconscious communication, 20–
      21
Underfunctioning, 28–30, 33, 34,
      37, 50, 82, 83, 88, 95, 99,
      117, 130
  chronic, 113
  overfunctioning vs., 100–2, 115
  partner response to, 88–90
  reciprocal (or circular)
      relationship pattern and,
      105–8
  sharing of, 177–78
  as stress management, 103, 121
Understanding, 40

Values, 209, 211
  clarification of, 220
  difference and, 71, 85
Violent behavior, 25
Vulnerability, 32, 33, 35, 51, 201
  anniversaries and, 49
  difficulty with expression of,
      101, 104
  sharing of, 104, 109–12, 178

Weaknesses. *See also* Vulnerability
  strengths vs., 11–12, 100–1
Willy. *See* Bill, Sue, and Willy
Worry, 90, 104, 115–16